Wicked
BOISE

Wicked BOISE

JANELLE M. SCHEFFELMAIER

THE
History
PRESS

Published by The History Press
Charleston, SC
www.historypress.com

Cover images: Idaho Capitol. *P775, "Boise Public Buildings—State Capitol," Idaho State Archives*; Boise, 1901. *P1973-75-2, "Boise Views, 1901," Idaho State Archives*; Idaho State Penitentiary inmate Fred Law, 1905. *AR42, Idaho State Penitentiary Collection, "Inmate 1184, Fred Law—A," Idaho State Archives.*

First published 2022

Manufactured in the United States

ISBN 9781467152228

Library of Congress Control Number: 2022933416

Notice: The information in this book is true and complete to the best of our knowledge. It is offered without guarantee on the part of the author or The History Press. The author and The History Press disclaim all liability in connection with the use of this book.

For Brylee.

Always remember "the most important thing."

No society has ever admitted that it could not sacrifice individual welfare to its own existence.

…Theory and fact agree in frequently punishing those who have been guilty of no moral wrong, and who could not be condemned by any standard that did not avowedly disregard the personal peculiarities of the individuals concerned.

…The law does undoubtedly treat the individual as a means to an end, and uses him as a tool to increase the general welfare at his own expense.

—Oliver Wendell Holmes, "The Common Law"

All men are by nature free and equal, and have certain inalienable rights, among which are enjoying and defending life and property; acquiring, possessing and protecting property; pursuing happiness and securing safety.

—Constitution of the State of Idaho

CONTENTS

CONTENTS

PREFACE

This is not a book I ever imagined myself writing. I am not a true crime buff nor a great crusader for law and order. What I am, though, is a historian interested in social constructs, the human condition, and the nuances that surround us. This is where the idea for *Wicked Boise* came from. I wanted to learn more about the everyday people affected by big ideas and events. I wanted to tell the stories of individuals whom history sometimes forgets—people like you and me who, but for some extraordinary circumstance or stroke of luck (good or bad), had their lives permanently altered. True crime—with its focus on misdeeds, unfortunate circumstances, and strong emotions—seemed like fertile ground to examine the complexity of human nature. *Wicked Boise*, I hope, illustrates that everyone and everything contains some level of integrity, dishonesty, good, and bad.

Wicked Boise simply would not have been possible without the support of many people. Thanks to the team at The History Press, specifically Artie Crisp, for having faith enough in my writing abilities to contact me about this project and answering all of my questions throughout the process.

I am always grateful for Ron Jackson, fellow Norwich alum and talented historian and writer, for his feedback, support, encouragement to follow my dreams, and reminders to work hard and use strong words.

Much gratitude to the staff of the Old Idaho Penitentiary and Idaho State Archives and Research Center. Erin Bostwick, Jim Riley, Amber Beierle, and Anthony Parry were quick to answer questions, share resources and reference materials and provide research advice.

Many thanks to Wine Coven members Mary Simons and Krista Mohn for their time and feedback to help shape and polish *Wicked Boise* into its final form.

Finally, thanks to my family and friends, who've always been an endless well of love and support in all my endeavors. Without you, I wouldn't be here, and I'm finally where I want to be.

Prologue

THE STOLEN CAPITAL

For generations, the Nez Perce Tribe called a large swath of land—more than 17 million acres—in the Inland Northwest home. The Nez Perce were traditionally nomadic, ranging mostly through what is now eastern Oregon and Washington and North-Central Idaho but traveling and engaging in trade with other indigenous peoples as far west as the Pacific Coast and east into Montana and Wyoming.* They fished in the waters of the Salmon, Snake, Clearwater, Columbia, and other rivers of the Northwest and hunted on the plains east of the Continental Divide. The Nez Perce have a rich cultural tradition and today may be most well known outside their lands for their skill raising horses. In just a century, the Nez Perce had built one of the largest horse herds on the North American continent. Their selective breeding practices—relatively uncommon in most indigenous cultures—created the Appaloosa breed.[1]

In the fall of 1805, Lewis and Clark's Corps of Discovery stumbled down the western slopes of the Rocky Mountains and met a band of the Nez Perce on the Clearwater River. The tribe provided the expedition with much-needed food and guidance and agreed to take care of the Corps' horses until they returned from their journey to the Pacific. The assistance of native peoples, like the Nez Perce, was integral to the Corps' survival and success—an idea that is often overlooked or downplayed in celebratory narratives about the expedition.

---

* Nez Perce is the name given to the tribe by French traders. The tribe's traditional name is Nimiipuu, meaning "The People."

Lewiston, Idaho, sits at the confluence of the Snake and Clearwater Rivers. Its deep port allows for barge access all the way to the Pacific. This made transporting supplies from Portland and other coastal cities to the nearby gold fields much easier. The site was an obvious choice for territorial capital. This photo was taken on a hill north of town in 1889. *P1963-4-1, "Lewiston—Views, 1889," Idaho State Archives.*

The Nez Perce lived in relative peace, occasionally encountering white explorers traveling through their lands. In 1860, though, gold was discovered in the mountains above the Clearwater River. Thousands of prospectors, merchants, traders, laborers, farmers, recent immigrants, and others poured into the rugged country around the Salmon, Snake, and Clearwater Rivers.

A spot on the valley floor, at the confluence of the Clearwater and Snake Rivers, was the perfect spot, the newcomers thought, to build a town. The deep inland port provided a convenient way to move goods and people to and from the Pacific Coast, and the valley's winters were mild in comparison to the bitter cold and deep snow in the surrounding mountains and high prairies. The population of this new city, called Lewiston after Meriwether Lewis, soon overshadowed that of Portland and Seattle combined. The Nez Perce soon found themselves fighting to maintain their traditional ways of life among this sudden deluge of newcomers.

More than two hundred miles to the south, the Northern Shoshone people were fighting a similar battle. The Northern Shoshones' ancestral lands

The Northern Shoshones lived a nomadic lifestyle, moving with the change in seasons. This Shoshone camp was taken after the tribe was settled onto the Fort Hall Reservation near Pocatello. *P1977-155-20a, "Shoshoni Indians Fort Hall Reservation," Idaho State Archives.*

spanned from northern Utah and Nevada, across portions of eastern and southern Idaho.* The Northern Shoshones adopted a Great Plains lifestyle, living nomadically and moving with the change in seasons. They fished for trout and salmon in Idaho's Salmon and Snake Rivers and their tributaries. The wide prairies provided camas bulbs and other valuable native plants. The buffalo, though, was the Northern Shoshones' "most significant source

---

* *Shoshone* is also often spelled *Shoshoni*. The name "Snake Indian" was also frequently used to identify the Shoshone people, based on the hand motion the Shoshones used for themselves in Native American sign language. The Shoshones use the term Newe, or "People," to refer to themselves. The Shoshones—including the Northern, Eastern and Western Shoshones—occupied an area stretching from northern Colorado across Wyoming, southern Idaho, northern Utah and Nevada and as far north as Montana and Canada.

of food and raw material." Each year, the Northern Shoshones, with their native neighbors, would mount their horses and travel across the Continental Divide into Montana for massive hunts. A good hunt could sustain the tribe through the year.[2]

Settlers passed through southern Idaho on the Oregon Trail, and some farmers and cattlemen stayed there, intent on settling the fertile Snake River Valley. With the 1862 discovery of gold in mountains north of present-day Boise, white miners also began to push into the tribe's ancestral territory. In 1863, the military established a small fort, Fort Boise, on the banks of the Boise River where the Oregon Trail crossed with the routes between rich southern Idaho gold deposits. The Northern Shoshones found themselves squeezed on all sides by white settlers. Natural grazing lands were fenced or plowed, and game sources grew scarce. The Northern Shoshones found it more difficult to travel across their plains and mountains undisturbed.[3]

In 1863, President Abraham Lincoln created Idaho Territory. He appointed William H. Wallace as governor. Lewiston, the territory's most populous settlement at the time, was a logical place for him to set up office. Wallace had all official territory business take place in Lewiston, and the territory's first legislative session was held there as well. During that first session, territorial legislators overlooked one very important detail: officially designating a territorial capital. Lewiston became the capital in name but not in deed.[4]

Wallace's time in Idaho was short. He left Lewiston after fewer than six months for Washington, D.C., to serve as the territory's House representative. The position of territorial governor remained open for nearly a year. Finally, in August 1864, President Lincoln appointed Caleb Lyon, a Republican from New York, to the position. Lyon had been in California during its gold rush and served as a secretary during that state's constitutional convention. At the time of his appointment, he was hoping for an appointment as minister to Bolivia. Instead, he ended up on a train bound west.[5]

By this time, gold had been discovered in the Boise Basin. The deposits in the mountains here were even richer than those in the north-central part of the territory. Idaho City, about forty-five miles north of Boise City, overtook Lewiston as Idaho Territory's largest settlement. The balance of power in the territory, many people thought, was shifting south. The American Civil War may have been drawing to a close in the East, but in Idaho, the territory's own civil war was just beginning.

Upon his arrival in Boise in August 1864, Governor Lyon was instantly beset by a group of men—the Boise delegation—that pushed on him the merits of Boise over Lewiston as the territorial capital. The delegation gave Lyon much to think about on his journey north to Lewiston and through the first weeks of his tenure.[6]

In November 1864, the second legislative session of Idaho Territory was also held in Lewiston. At this session, the northern representatives found themselves sorely outnumbered. They attempted to avoid discussion of the capital location, instead entreating Congress to create a new territory with northern Idaho and eastern Washington. Southern Idaho, then, could be left to its own devices. Southern delegates disagreed, though. On December 24, they pushed a vote on the capital and soundly defeated the northerners. Lyon signed it immediately.[7]

The northerners were, of course, outraged. They took the matter to court. The whole legislative session, they argued, was illegal. Since the first session had passed conflicting laws on session timing, the second session had started on the wrong day. Indeed, they continued, no one even knew which day was the right one to begin. A Lewiston lawyer argued that "sundry persons claiming to have been elected as members of the House of Representatives' had met before their terms commenced and 'pretended' to locate the capital permanently in Boise." The northern lawyers were able to have a court order drawn up and signed to prevent anyone—politician or plunderer— from removing the territorial seal and archives from the Lewiston capitol building. The Lewiston delegation went yet a step further and had another order drawn up forbidding Governor Lyon from leaving Lewiston. However, Lyon, ever the politician, used his "persuasive and flattering tongue, which at times served him in the absence of sincerity and ability," to beg for a short release from his confinement to go duck hunting. His request was granted. Instead of hunting ducks, though, Lyon took the opportunity to flee to Walla Walla, Washington. He never returned.[8]

The people of Lewiston didn't celebrate Lyon's disappearing act as victory, though. Six armed men were assigned to protect the seal and archives. This proved necessary when they stopped an attempt the Boise delegation made to take them on the final day of 1864.[9]

Clinton DeWitt Smith was named the next acting governor of Idaho Territory. Smith arrived in Idaho in early 1865 and was initially well liked in Lewiston. He was "jovial [and] hard-drinking" and more relatable than the untrustworthy New Yorker Lyon had been. One can easily imagine Smith sharing a round or two of whiskey with the locals. The mood quickly turned against Smith, though, when he spoke out about his preference for Boise as the capital.[10]

Left: Clinton DeWitt Smith was appointed acting governor of Idaho Territory after Caleb Lyon's disappearing act. Described as "jovial [and] hard-drinking," Smith was initially quite popular with the people of Lewiston. He was eventually responsible for the theft of the territorial seal and archives from Lewiston and establishment of the capital at Boise. *P1979-2-23, "Clinton deWitt Smith," Idaho State Archives.*

Right: The Idaho Territorial Seal was based on a design by Caleb Lyon. After it was stolen, it was used briefly on territorial documents until it disappeared for good sometime in or after 1879. *P1963-5-18c, "Idaho Territorial Seals," Idaho State Archives.*

Ultimately, Smith, in the eyes of northerners, proved even more underhanded and deceptive than Lyon. On March 29, 1865, just weeks after his arrival in Idaho, Smith saddled up his horse for his daily ride. He headed south to Fort Lapwai but didn't return that day. Instead, he rode back into Lewiston a day later with a military escort. In defiance of the earlier court order, Smith, with the help of his armed guard, overpowered the Lewiston delegate's citizen guard, took the territorial seal and the archives and rode hard for Boise. The seal and archives were immediately secured. One year later, in 1866, the new Idaho Territorial Supreme Court upheld the legislative vote and ruled that Boise was the capital "in law and fact."[11] Lewiston's supporters had no further recourse. As quickly as it had begun, the battle for the capital had been lost.

The territorial seal was used on official documents from 1863 to 1866 and again from 1877 to 1879 but never again. The seal has been missing ever since.[12]

Clinton DeWitt Smith's infamous act of larceny solidified Idaho's rivalry between north and south; it's a feud that this author—a North Idaho native living and working in southern Idaho—can attest still exists to this day.

Back in North-Central Idaho and eastern Oregon, the Nez Perce attempted to live peacefully with their new white neighbors. Ultimately, though, as more and more European settlers poured into the area, tensions grew. In 1877, the U.S. government ordered the tribe to leave their various homes and move onto the reservation at Lapwai, south of Lewiston. They refused. After several battles and an epic and courageous flight across parts of Idaho and Montana, the tribe surrendered to the U.S. Army and moved onto 770,000 acres at Lapwai, a tiny fraction of their traditional lands. In the generations since, tribal members have dedicated an extraordinary amount of time and resources toward preservation of their traditional ways of life and natural resource stewardship, caring for their beloved lands and rivers.[13]

In southern Idaho, the Northern Shoshones also pushed back against white encroachment, leading to some violent clashes. In January 1863, the U.S. Army massacred between 250 and 400 Shoshone people in southeastern Idaho. This atrocity was one of many that culminated in the Snake War, a four-year affair characterized by guerrilla-style warfare. Bands of Shoshones and Paiutes fought the U.S. Army in Oregon, California, Nevada, and Idaho. The conflict drew to an end in 1868 following peace talks, but by this time, more than 1,700 had lost their lives. The Northern Shoshones moved to the reservation at Fort Hall, Idaho, after the Fort Bridger Treaty was signed in 1868. Originally 1.8 million acres in size, allotment and other legislation reduced the reservation to its current size—just over 500,000 acres. Today, the Shoshone-Bannock Tribes are dedicated to preserving their culture and language.* The tribes have several programs dedicated to preserving and illuminating Shoshone-Bannock culture and history for future generations. They are also active participants in land conservation and stewardship efforts both on and off the reservation, throughout their traditional lands.[14]

Today, the City of Trees is generally known for its beauty, economic soundness, safe neighborhoods, and overall livability. The Treasure Valley is one of the fastest-growing and desirable areas in the United States. This doesn't mean, though, that Boise doesn't have a few skeletons in its closet. The thievery and deception that made Boise the state's capital was only the beginning.†

---

* The Shoshone-Bannock Tribes are made up of Northern Shoshones and the Bannock bank of Northern Paiutes.

† There are five federally recognized tribes in Idaho. Along with the Nez Perce and Shoshone-Bannocks are the Kootenai Tribe and Coeur d'Alene Tribe in North Idaho and Shoshone-Paiutes on the border of Idaho and Nevada. This is nowhere near an exhaustive list of all the indigenous peoples who passed through, lived in and have cultural connections to Idaho. A wonderful resource for beginning to learn more about the traditional lands and languages of the indigenous peoples of what is now is the United States is www.native-land.ca.

Part I

LEGAL LAWBREAKERS

The Vigilance Committees of Southern Idaho

Yankees and Rebels in Idaho City

Nestled in the mountains approximately forty miles north of Boise sits the small, quiet hamlet of Idaho City. Today, Idaho City has about five hundred permanent residents. But in the early 1860s, the town was one of the West's busiest places. It was also one of the deadliest.

In the mid-1800s, white prospectors and explorers began to hear stories about "gold nuggets so plentiful they could be scooped up by the handful" on the banks of the streams and creeks of the Boise Basin.* The California Gold Rush, just a little more than a decade before, was still fresh in their minds, and the possibilities that lay in the Idaho mountains were tantalizing. George Grimes, a native New Yorker who was then in Walla Walla, decided to find out if the stories were true. In the summer of 1862, he and a party of prospectors set out for the rugged mountains of Central Idaho. The journey was incredibly difficult. The terrain was steep, rough and unforgiving. The area hadn't been mapped yet. Even in the summer, nights in the mountains could be bitterly cold. Supplies had to be packed in on mules and the party's backs. A camp guard kept watch for bears, mountain lions and other wild

---

* The Boise Basin refers to the vast area of mountain creeks and streams that drain into the Boise River. The Boise Basin encompasses about three hundred square miles of rugged mountainous land north of present-day Boise, Idaho. More gold was removed from the Boise Basin than from the California or Klondike Gold Rushes.

animals at night. The possibility of attacks by Native Americans—the area's only inhabitants—was never far from the men's minds.[15]

In August, after climbing and descending peak after peak, crossing numerous icy creeks and traversing boulder-strewn valleys, Grimes and his party found gold—a lot of it. Just days later, the party was set on by a band of Shoshone-Bannocks. The Shoshone-Bannocks had been driven into the mountains after emigrant wagon trains and settlers in the lower river valleys had depleted their resources. Upon finding yet another group of invading white people in their lands, they attacked. Grimes was killed in the skirmish.* Today, a creek and a mountain pass in the Boise Basin bear his name.[16]

The survivors trickled back out of the mountains, taking stories of rich gold deposits with them, using the gold flakes and nuggets they'd found as evidence. People began pouring into the Boise Basin. Idaho City sprang up and boomed, quickly overtaking Lewistown as the largest settlement in the Northwest. By 1863, Idaho City's population was about six thousand. Within three years, the total population of the Boise Basin numbered between fifteen thousand and thirty thousand people. More than 250 businesses had opened their doors in Idaho City.† Livery stables, a factory, banks, groceries and dry goods stores, dance halls, saloons, and even an opera house grew up around the miners' tents and shanties.[17]

Idaho City was rough and wild. Carved out of the rugged mountains and settled by men as wild as the wilderness itself, Idaho City was "ruled by guns and gold." Within a year, two hundred graves lined the cemetery. All but twenty-eight held men who had died of gunshot wounds. To say Idaho City was tough was an understatement. Idaho City was unruly, dangerous, and exciting—a city that could either help a man make his fortune or put him in an early grave.[18]

Such a place needed law and order, and Sumner Pinkham was the man chosen to bring that to Idaho City. Pinkham arrived in Idaho Territory in 1862 from the gold fields of California. Standing an imposing six feet, two inches tall and sporting a thick beard, Pinkham certainly had the look of a rough frontiersman. He was loud and opinionated, "very noisy, when in liquor…very insulting, too, at times." However, he could also be "a very positive man…socially kind and obliging."[19]

---

* Present-day Idaho is, by and large, a great supporter of the Second Amendment. It is not uncommon to hear Idahoans speak openly about their willingness to defend their homes and property from invaders and thieves by whatever means necessary, just as the Shoshone-Bannocks did.
† Like all booms, the Boise Basin's did come to an end. Today, mounds of dirt and rock line the area's roadways and creek banks, a callback to the early days of gold mining in the basin.

By the mid-1860s, Idaho City had become the largest city in the Northwest. This photo shows Idaho City in 1875, less than ten years after the initial gold rush and before the boom ultimately came to an end. *P1966-74-86, "Idaho City circa 1875," Idaho State Archives.*

Originally from Illinois, Pinkham was also a "staunch but radical Unionist" in an area thickly populated with Confederate sympathizers.[20] He was "intolerant and bigoted in his way." His barbs were aimed mainly at his political opponents, whom he openly and loudly referred to as "'Copperheads,' 'rebels,' and 'traitors.'"[21] With the closest battlefields more than a thousand miles away, the Civil War may have seemed a distant conflict. However, the political divisions in the East were also apparent in the remote wilderness of the Boise Basin. Idaho Territory may have been bound to the laws and principles of the Constitution, but its distance from the Union proper drew hundreds, if not thousands, of Confederate sympathizers and secessionists. Idaho's remoteness and vast spaces, these men believed, were a blank canvas on which to create a region that preserved the rights of men and states to live as they pleased, not as dictated by the Union. These Southern Democrats were wildly popular candidates for political office in the territory. The *Idaho Statesman* provided a rousing endorsement for a Boise County judge to a man who "makes the longest and loudest pro-slavery speeches of all the men of his party." This attitude would render him "entirely powerless" in Washington, D.C., where his politics were opposed. Idahoans, though, the *Statesman* proclaimed, would be fortunate to have him in local office.[22]

Pinkham's politics may have made him an outlier in Idaho City, but he made up for that with his fair reputation. The same *Statesman* writer who endorsed the proslavery judge claimed that Pinkham, a Republican, "discharged his duties to all the people, irrespective of party." The

"democratic party," the writer continued, had elected "a sheriff before Pinkham that let every felon go scot free."[23] The people of Idaho City agreed that Pinkham was the best choice, and he was elected sheriff of Boise County, headquartered in the rough-and-tumble town.*

Pinkham knew that he was outnumbered by his political and ideological rivals, but rather than be intimidated, he reveled in their frequent, usually harmless, clashes. He organized a Fourth of July parade through the center of Idaho City and marched behind a drummer and fifer—whom he'd paid out of his own pocket—waving a Union flag. He bought rounds of drinks for the "Johnny Rebs" in the saloons and then made them listen to him sing renditions of Union songs.[24] Most of Idaho City's residents found this harmless behavior slightly irritating or amusing. A few people, though, took serious offence.

Pinkham quickly made himself an enemy in F.J. "Ferd" Patterson. A southerner—born in Tennessee and raised in Texas and Louisiana—Patterson also made his way to Idaho City by way of California. The reasons behind his move, though, were much different than Pinkham's. Patterson was no miner but, rather, a gambler by trade. The appearance, mannerisms, and charm necessary for success at the high-roller tables were a perfect match for his rich, southern plantation upbringing. Gambling, though, especially at the stakes Patterson played at, was a job almost as dangerous as mining. With just one unlucky hand, a man could find a pistol in his face. For a man with a high temper, the odds of that happening were even higher. Ferd Patterson was that type of high-tempered man, and after a tense encounter at a Sacramento card table, Patterson found himself unwelcome in California. He boarded a ship toward Portland. There, Patterson was accused of killing a Captain Staples, a "sad affair… the wind-up of a drunken debauch."[25] No longer welcome in Portland either, Patterson made his way to the Boise Basin, turning toward the West's latest literal and proverbial gold mine for his next big take.[26]

---

* Until late 1864, Boise County encompassed much of the entire Boise Basin and Treasure Valley, including present-day Ada and Canyon Counties. Idaho City was the county seat and largest settlement in the area. Ada County was formed in December 1864, and Canyon split from Ada in 1891.

Opposite: Sumner Pinkham was a northern Republican and supporter of the Union and Abraham Lincoln. These views were not always popular in Idaho Territory, which had become something of a haven for Confederate sympathizers and secessionists. Nevertheless, Pinkham's fairness and jovial nature made him a popular figure in Idaho City. *Album G1, P249-29, "Biography—Sumner Pinkham," Idaho State Archives.*

Right: Born in Tennessee and from Texas and Louisiana, gambler Ferd Patterson dressed himself in the style of a southern gentleman. He was well dressed, charming, and affable, but he had a quick temper and reckless streak. *P111b, "Biography—Ferd Patterson," Idaho State Archives.*

Patterson stepped into Idaho City, and men immediately took notice. He was certainly a striking physical figure, standing more than six feet and sporting sandy hair, a well-trimmed beard, and bright blue eyes that seemed to notice everything. Patterson was well dressed, wearing silk and plaid, a heavy gold watch chain, heeled and polished boots, and a long frock coat. His pale skin made it even further apparent that he spent little time outdoors, and the revolver and Bowie knife at his side boasted ivory handles, better for ornamentation than practical use. The other displaced Southerners and Confederate sympathizers of Idaho City quickly looked to Patterson as their de facto leader. With two men with such conflicting appearance, ideologies, mannerisms, and values leading the factions in Idaho City, it is not surprising that this frontier town, more than 2,300 miles from Virginia, found itself in the midst of its own civil war shortly after Lee's surrender at Appomattox.[27]

Pinkham and Patterson had their first run-in sometime in the winter of 1864–65. The reason for their disagreement is unknown. Perhaps Patterson didn't find one of Pinkham's pro-Union antics amusing. Maybe the men had a contentious encounter over a card table. Their relationship was certainly marred by various minor run-ins and disagreements, accumulating growing resentment and anger over time. Animosity, especially on Patterson's side, grew. The gambler spent months plotting, formulating a plan behind his best expressionless poker face.[28]

Sunday afternoons found many of Idaho City's residents at Warm Springs, located just a mile and a half down the road from the mining town. Tired miners would gather to soothe their sore muscles in the natural warm pools; place friendly, and sometimes unfriendly, bets at the card tables; enjoy a few glasses of whiskey; or share the company of a "working woman." Pinkham found nothing out of the ordinary to accept an invitation to Warm Springs, and on July 23, 1865, he rode down to, he believed, look over some horses. Much more was in store.[29]

Eyewitness testimony can be unreliable. Human memory is fallible and can be modified to fit the narrative presented and molded to better represent the witness or other parties involved. Eyewitness testimony, though, is all that was available to determine exactly what happened that hot July day at Warm Springs.

Pinkham arrived at Warm Springs in high spirits. He swaggered into the bar singing "We'll Hang Jeff Davis on a Sour Apple Tree." As he sat to have a drink, Pinkham gaily began offering bets that "Jeff Davis would be hung and all his sympathizers." At some point, the mood turned. Perhaps he spotted Patterson looking murderous, enraged by his pro-Union comments. Maybe he heard whispers. Whatever the case, at some point that afternoon, Pinkham realized that the time for his final showdown with Patterson had arrived. He stepped out of the saloon and posted himself by the stair rail. "Look out," he reportedly told a man named Cole as the latter made his way up the steps into the saloon. Pinkham remained outside.[30]

According to witnesses at the scene, Patterson had a swim and then a drink at the bar. After gulping his whiskey, Patterson made a pronouncement. Some witnesses heard, "I will kill the d--d s-n of-a-b----." Others heard Patterson swear that he would "get some of the d--d s--s of b-----s yet." Either way, Patterson's intentions were clear as he slammed his empty glass on the bar and stalked toward the door.[31]

Those inside the barroom strained their ears to hear what happened next. Again, witnesses disagreed on the exact words Patterson used to antagonize Pinkham.

"Don't you draw."

"You will draw, will you?"

"You will draw on me, you old son -----."

Pinkham replied, but his words were unclear. Shots rang out. Some witnesses reported hearing two shots. Others said three or four. One claimed to hear five. The first two shots, they all agreed, came in quick succession.[32]

Investigation revealed that two of the chambers in Pinkham's pistol were empty. The sheriff had managed to get off a shot or two at Patterson. A few men claimed to have seen everything. Pinkham, they agreed, drew first. The lawman's pistol snapped but didn't fire. "There were but three shots," an eyewitness reported, "the first was fired by Patterson—the other two I only heard."[33]

Patterson mounted a horse and spurred it quickly down the road. "If you hear anyone inquiring for me," he told a witness on his way, "tell them that I am leaving the country for killing old Pink."[34] Pinkham's associates gave chase and caught Patterson before he made it halfway to Boise, where he could catch a stage or a fresh horse to ride for freedom. Patterson was taken back to Idaho City and placed in jail.[35]

Outrage spread throughout the Boise Basin. Pinkham's murder illustrated "the enormity of the riot of crime that [ran] loose in Idaho."[36] "There are evils," an editorialist wrote in Idaho City's *Idaho World*, "which sometimes accumulate until they can no longer be borne—for which there is no redress, and to which there is apparently [*sic*] no termination. The right of revolution, the last recourse of society, as the right of self-defense, is of the individual—under such circumstances may then be resorted to, and would be justified by the moral sense of the community."[37] A Vigilance Committee was this "last recourse of society." A writer with Boise's *Idaho Statesman* agreed. "This most atrocious affair is only one of a number of circumstances lately transpiring that tend to show that there is a determination on the part of a band of men in Boise county to rule it with the knife and bullet. It is about time for that kind of rule to come to an end—a rope's end."[38] The vigilance-minded men of Idaho City called on a young man named William McConnell to help them.[39]

McConnell was the founder of the Payette Vigilance Committee, a group of men based in the Payette Valley around present-day Emmett who were determined to save their livestock and livelihood from thieves by whatever means necessary. McConnell shared the by-laws and guidelines that had been adopted by his Payette Vigilantes with the interested men of the Boise Basin. "A few men of the entire population," he stated, "had been able to perpetrate most of the crimes." A group of brave and upright citizens, then, should have little trouble organizing enough to take back their towns and settlements and bring justice to perhaps not only the Boise Basin and Payette Valley but all of Idaho Territory. Under McConnell's tutelage, the Idaho City Vigilance Committee was founded. Within two weeks, its membership rolls exceeded nine hundred men.[40]

Rumors began to fly around Idaho City. The vigilantes, the town's state-sanctioned lawmen heard, planned to "assault the jail." Their goal was to liberate Ferd Patterson in order to ensure that he could not escape punishment for his crime and that true justice would be served. Idaho City's new sheriff and his deputies immediately made their own counterplans. They gathered arms and ammunition and formed a vigilance committee of their own—"a posse of citizens summoned for defense."[41]

On Friday, September 1, 1865, heavily armed men from throughout the Boise Basin rode into Idaho City. The town's residents prepared for war. "Many business men removed their goods from their stores…the jail was prepared for an assault or a siege, and the times appeared dangerous."[42]

The vigilantes mounted their offense in the hills just west of the jail, and the sheriff's party gathered around the building in defense. Through the night, "both parties made frequent reconnoisances [sic] to feel each other." Small parties of men, rifles and pistols at the ready, dodged through the shadows in and around Idaho City all night while the townspeople huddled in their darkened homes, waiting anxiously for the pops and snaps of gunfire and the rumbling of homemade explosives.[43]

The tense night passed in relative quiet, though. The sheriff's men captured a few of the vigilante scouting parties, and at daybreak most of the vigilantes dispersed. The sheriff and his supporters, though, knew that the situation was not over. On Sunday, men again began to gather just outside of town with "unfriendly designs." They rode through the hills, dodging the sheriff and his men. Finally, exhausted by hard riding through rugged terrain, both groups of law and order men met to discuss terms.[44]

William McConnell served as representative for the Idaho City Vigilance Committee. His was an unenviable position. The Idaho City Vigilance Committee—the group he had helped create—wanted justice. Patterson's connections in Idaho City all but ensured that a trial verdict would acquit him. However, McConnell knew that many in Idaho City feared the Vigilance Committee's potential. Despite early support for vigilante justice, an *Idaho World* writer now warned that continued vigilance activity would result in "conflagrations and civil war…engulfing the lives and property of thousands of men and women having no connection with it."[45] Perhaps McConnell felt pressured by the people of Idaho City—those with no involvement in the

The first territorial prison was built in Idaho City in 1864. The standoff between William McConnel's vigilantes and the sheriff's posse took place on the mountainsides around the jail. *P113, "Idaho City Prisons—Idaho Penitentiary," Idaho State Archives.*

Patterson-Pinkham fray—to put a quick and clean end to the whole affair. An argument over justice, loyalties, and political views was the flashpoint for all of the activity. Pinkham, many believed, "was assassinated because he was an unyielding and fearless Union man, whose presence the terrorists of Boise county could not longer suffer."[46] There must be an end to the continued public, politically driven violence. A truce, McConnell decided, was the best way to end another civil war before it began.

McConnell assured the sheriff that if he agreed to let the vigilantes disperse peacefully without fear of retribution, they would allow Patterson to go to trial peacefully. The bargain was struck, and all returned to their homes and hung up their weapons. A few weeks later, Patterson was tried and, just as McConnell predicted, was acquitted of Pinkham's murder. Patterson left the Boise Basin immediately. "Ferd Patterson, who made his name memorable in Idaho, has left the territory for his old home at the East," the *Idaho World* reported shortly after his acquittal.[47]

The members of Idaho City Vigilance Committee were outraged. "The Vigilance movement would have been a success if we had not been fool enough to admit two or three Democrats into the organization," one bitter member stated.[48] Maybe, they thought, McConnell had been swayed by someone who, like Patterson, did not appreciate Pinkham's politics or his brash way of asserting them. This was unlikely, though. McConnell, like Pinkham, was a Republican. Perhaps McConnell, in a calculated move, had other plans.

Despite the *Idaho World*'s report, Patterson did not return east. A few months later, in February 1866, news from Walla Walla, Washington, reported the "cold-blooded murder" of Ferd Patterson. As Patterson sat in a barber's chair having a shave, a man named Donahue came in the back door. Donahue was a policeman, so witnesses thought he meant to arrest Patterson. However, rather than pulling handcuffs from his belt, Donahue pulled a pistol. "Patterson, you must kill me, or I'll kill you!" Donahue reportedly shouted and fired before Patterson had a chance to react.[49]

The shot hit Patterson in the face. He immediately jumped up. "Oh, my God!" Patterson exclaimed, staggering toward the door. Donahue fired again. His misplaced aim shattered the barber's window. He fired a third time. This shot hit Patterson in the back. The wounded man made his way to a neighboring saloon and collapsed in the doorway. Donahue followed and towered above him. He looked down and fired twice more, each ball hitting its target. His work complete, Donahue immediately turned himself in.[50]

Donahue's motives were unclear. Some claimed that Donahue and Patterson "had a difficulty in Portland a year or two since, and the killing was the result of an old grudge." Others said the disagreement was more recent and that the two men had quarreled just the night before. Friends of Patterson, though, had another theory altogether. Patterson and Donahue were "entire strangers," they said, with no prior knowledge of one another. Patterson's "assassination was a part of a deliberate plan to get him out of the way."[51]

The jury was unable to agree on a verdict, and Donahue was remanded to jail until another trial could be scheduled. That trial would never take place. Donahue escaped from prison a short time later. His escape, though, the *Walla Walla Statesman* proclaimed, was not a mistake at all. Donahue had been released from prison. He was captured in September in San Francisco, bearing a certificate claiming that he had been tried and acquitted for the murder of Ferd Patterson. The certificate allegedly bore the signature of the governor of Washington Territory and some influential Walla Walla residents.[52]

Who had orchestrated Donahue's release and granted him an unofficial pardon for the murder of Patterson? No responsible party was ever formally identified, but one man did take credit. William McConnell seems to have had a plan when he had the Idaho City Vigilance Committee step down after all. Donahue, he said, "had been hired by the Vigilantes committee to shoot Ferd [Patterson] down like a dog without giving him a chance."[53] In the minds of the vigilantes, justice had, in the end, been done.

The *Walla Walla Statesman*, in arguing against Donahue's secret release, unwittingly justified the vigilante view:

> *It is the duty of every good citizen to protect himself and the community, and no one should evade the responsibility when it presents itself in such a shape as the open question which is now before the people of Walla Walla county, to wit; shall the laws be enforced and criminals brought to justice? Or shall legal proceedings become a farce and murderers and their abettors defeat judicial proceedings, and sneer at legal restraints or responsibilities?*[54]

STOLEN HORSES AND FAKE GOLD

The Boise Basin promised riches not only for the miners who found gold and silver in its mountains but also for the farmers and ranchers who settled the wide-open spaces of the Boise, Payette, and Snake River Valleys. But where men seek to make futures for themselves based on hard work, perseverance and a little luck, thieves, bandits, and outlaws of all types look to do the same by more dishonest means. Idaho Territory was not just a haven for men trying to avoid service in the Civil War and disaffected Confederate sympathizers like those in Idaho City. Malcontents who'd defected or been banished from emigrant groups on the Oregon, California, and Mormon Trails and others who made their way from settlement to settlement throughout the West seeking their next payday, however it may come, also roamed throughout Idaho Territory.

Travelers were the most likely targets for thieves out for a quick score. Men flush with riches from the mines of Idaho City to the north and Silver City and the Owyhees to the south descended on Boise to catch the stage to take them to larger cities like Salt Lake City, Denver, San Francisco, or

Portland. One of these men was William H. Parks, former sheriff of Baker City, Oregon, and, during the Idaho gold rush, a mine operator with holdings outside Silver City. Parks joined a group headed east on the Overland Stage in the early morning hours of Tuesday, November 8, 1864.[55]

The stage had only traveled a few miles—still within the present-day Boise city limits—when it was overtaken by a group of men. In a sequence of events replayed today in western movies, a small party of armed, masked men jumped in front of the stage, shouting for the driver to stop. Inside the stage, the two passengers, Parks and a man named Harmer, both drew their pistols to defend themselves and their possessions. In the process, Harmer's already cocked pistol hit his holster and went off. A deafening crack filled the stage, and gunpowder filled the air. When it cleared, Parks was clutching his hip. Blood seeped through his fingers.[56]

The shot stopped the defense of the stage but not the robbery. The masked men, in voices "more emphatic than polite," ordered the driver to unhitch the team. The driver had his hands tied behind him and was searched for money and other valuables. When his pockets turned up empty, the thieves pulled the stage's occupants, including the bleeding Parks, out into the predawn twilight. Two or three of them roughly tied and searched the travelers, while others waited in the bushes by the road, guns trained on the stage and the hostages. The travelers' pockets and cases were emptied of cash, coin, and gold dust and discarded empty along the side of the road. "You are a d----d poor crowd," said one of the robbers, unhappy with the small take. "Driver you ought to be ashamed of hauling so poor a crowd." Then the thieves turned to Park, accusing him of hiding more than they'd found on his person. Park simply stood quietly holding his hip, faint from blood loss.[57]

Though displeased with the outcome of their venture, the masked men seemed content to stop at robbery rather than proceeding to murder. They ordered the driver to hitch the team back up and keep driving. They denied the driver's request to return to town with the injured Parks. Then they rode off into the early morning toward Boise. The driver continued east a few more miles, allowing the thieves to get a head start. Then he crossed the river and took a different road back to the city.[58]

The stage pulled back into Boise, and Parks received medical attention. His wound wasn't serious, and he survived to tell the tale, as well as brag that he'd outwitted the gang—even after he'd been shot, "he was still able to secret a purse of over $300 in gold in the coach, and a slug worth $225 in his clothes" while the thieves were searching the driver and other passengers. The thieves

Stagecoach robberies were, unfortunately, not a rare occurrence in Idaho Territory. This scene, photographed outside of Lewiston, is probably very similar to the one that occurred outside Boise in the early morning of November 8, 1864. *P3793-24, "Stage Coaches—Stage 'Hold Up,'" Idaho State Archives.*

had been right after all—Park had been holding out on them. But how did they know? Shortly after the crime was reported, two men suspected of playing a part in the robbery were arrested. One of them was Harmer, the passenger who'd *accidentally* shot Parks. The other men were never arrested, but rumors and suspicions of their identities flew around Boise.[59]

Those same suspects were part of a group that made their dishonest living in various other nefarious ways common in the Old West. The Pickett Corral Gang ran a counterfeit gold dust operation, stole goods from pack trains, rustled cattle, and stole horses. The gang was responsible for the theft of hundreds, perhaps thousands of horses in the Snake, Payette, and Boise River Valleys. They drove herds to temporary hiding places in the trees along the banks of the Boise River or to a pickett corral (unironically how the group earned its name) in the canyon between Emmett and Horseshoe Bend. From there, the horses were driven across the Territory border to sell in Nevada, Oregon, and California.[60]

The Pickett Corral Gang was unfortunately good at what it did. "Horse stealing must be reduced to a science in this country; that is, in the popular phrase, defies competition and almost detection," the *Idaho Statesman* proclaimed in June 1865.[61] One writer claimed that only one horse out of the thousands stolen in Idaho Territory's first three years was ever found and returned to its owner. Although the veracity of that claim cannot be completely proven, it still illustrates just how rampant and near-impossible the crime was to prosecute. The recovered horse in question belonged to William McConnell. Before he helped found Idaho's first vigilance committees, McConnell was a farmer with a small plot just outside Horseshoe Bend, not far from the Pickett Corral Gang's hiding place. He grew vegetables to sell to miners. The vegetable business was a surprisingly lucrative one. Vegetables were hard to come by in the rugged mountains of Central Idaho. Most had to be shipped from Portland and packed into the mining camps. By the time the goods reached their destination, their freshness had expired by days, even weeks. As such, McConnell's local goods brought high prices. His cucumbers sold for two dollars apiece and his corn for twelve dollars per dozen—high prices even today. McConnell, though, had one big problem: his horses and mules kept going missing.[62]

Livestock were expensive, and McConnell wasn't about to let his disappear without at least an extensive search. Eventually, one of his searches proved fruitful. In August 1864, McConnell found one of his mares, missing from his pasture for two months, in a Boise livery stable owned by David C. Updyke, a man with many friends and no shortage of influence in the city.

Though not one of the horses he'd been looking for—those would never be recovered—McConnell was more than happy to find the rogue mare. Getting her back, though, wasn't so easy. The mare, a judge ruled, no longer belonged to McConnell. Without evidence that her new owner had stolen her, McConnell had to pay not only the back costs for the horse's board at Updyke's stable but also the court fees just to get his mare back. In total, reclaiming his property cost McConnell more than seventy dollars in gold.[63]

Incensed and seething, McConnell stood outside the courthouse in Boise and swore an oath against any man who stole from him again. Next time, "there would be no law suits [*sic*]."[64] The justice of the law, McConnell felt, had failed him; the next time, he would administer justice himself.

Not a week passed before McConnell's oath, seen as a challenge to some, was tested. Five of the farmer's horses, along with four mules valued at more than $2,000, were stolen from his property. McConnell wasted no time. He and three other armed men, with an extra horse apiece, followed the trail left by the rustlers down the valley, across the Snake River, and into Oregon. They caught the criminals near La Grande. A shootout left four of the thieves dead and the fifth in custody. McConnell and his crew turned the surviving thief over to the La Grande authorities "after confessions and names of all the rest of the members of the organization were obtained, and of course after he had been shot."[65] McConnell had made good on his vow.

McConnell and his partners returned to the Payette Valley with the recovered horses and mules nearly a month after leaving. Upon his return, McConnell called the men living in the valley for a meeting. Each of them, he knew, was frustrated and tired of the thievery and lawlessness that ran, seemingly unchecked, throughout the region. With no law enforcement to protect their property and interests, the men took matters upon themselves. Forty men showed up at McConnell's meeting, and together they drafted and adopted two resolutions:

> *(1st:) To stand as a unit on all matters affecting the personal safety or the property rights of any individual resident.*
>
> *(2nd:) To pursue and capture, regardless of expense, all horsethieves* [sic] *who thereafter appropriated any horses, cattle or mules, belonging to any individual resident or traveler passing through that section. Provided, that after the capture was made, the posse affecting it should administer such condign punishment as in their judgement the circumstances merited— always bearing in mind that farmers were not prepared to hold prisoners.*[66]

Where the thieves had found strength in numbers, so would McConnell and the other men of the Payette Valley. Their resources would be pooled to protect one another's property and livelihoods, and rather than make the long ride to the nearest jail, the men would administer their own swift justice in order to carry on with their lives and business. Thus, led by twenty-five-year-old McConnell, the Payette Vigilance Committee was formed in 1864. Idaho's "first large-scale law and order group" saw its authority grow outside of the Payette Valley, throughout the Treasure Valley, across the Snake River, and beyond. In a short time, its influence extended from Walla Walla in the northwest across southern Idaho to the Montana border in the east.[67]

Although deterring cattle rustling and horse theft was the primary impetus for many of the men who joined the Payette Vigilance Committee, the group's first major strike for law and order was the breakup of a counterfeiting operation that threatened Boise's economic stability. The currency of choice in southern Idaho in the 1860s was gold. After the coveted mineral was discovered in the mountains of the Boise Basin, businessmen preferred to deal in gold rather than silver.

Despite the number of rich deposits in the area, many men found that counterfeiting gold was much easier than prospecting. In fact, with just a small bit of gold, a chunk of lead and a bit of ingenuity, an enterprising man could more than double the value of his investment. The counterfeiter cut the cheap lead into small, manageable pieces and, through a galvanizing process utilizing just a small bit of his real gold, could turn the lead into a product that looked like rich gold dust.[68] Other counterfeiters took an easier route. They simply mixed some gold dust with actual dust—"with sand, with Alturas and Owyhee dust, with dust from the mills, and with dust of every description" until most of the mass was a worthless pile of dirt.[69] The massive amounts of "spurious and adulterated dust put into circulation" seriously "depreciated the average standard value of Boise gold dust."[70] A number of men surely arrived at a bank in Denver, Chicago, or San Francisco only to find that their cases full of riches were actually worth a mere fraction of what they'd anticipated.

The details are scarce, but McConnell and his Payette Vigilance Committee were reportedly involved in exposing and breaking up of one of the largest counterfeit operations in the Treasure Valley. The leader of the operation, a man named Conklin, was ordered to leave Idaho Territory within twenty-four hours of his sentencing. As one of the men mainly responsible for the downfall of the counterfeiting operation, McConnell was charged with ensuring that the sentence was carried out. Rather than wait for the vigilante leader to come and meet him, though, Conklin and a handful of supporters rode out from Pickett's Corral to the site of present-day Emmett, where McConnell had lodged overnight at a roadhouse. The two men recognized each other instantly. When Conklin asked McConnell for a word outside, the vigilante strapped on his guns before walking out the door.

Outside, Conklin and his men backed McConnell against a corral wall. McConnell, though, showed the same courage and spirit that had allowed him to successfully retrieve his stolen horses. "Men, show your colors," he reportedly said. "I will make this the biggest funeral ever held in this valley. I know you: I understand what this means. You are here to murder me, but I don't think you can do it."[71]

Conklin and his men were very well aware of McConnell's reputation. No doubt, these

William McConnell's youthful looks belied his tough and assertive demeanor. McConnell founded both the Payette and Idaho City Vigilance Committees. Among his vigilante accomplishments is the dissolution of a large gold counterfeiting operation that threatened the plunge southern Idaho's economy into ruins. *P1974-190-1, "Biography—William J. McConnel," Idaho State Archives.*

words reminded them of those McConnell uttered and followed through on outside of the courthouse in Boise. No shots were fired. Conklin, however, refused to take the paper order McConnell thrust in front of him. Undeterred yet again, McConnell read the order out loud to ensure that it was delivered. One can imagine that as soon as he'd finished reading the order, McConnell again put his hands to his gun belt, daring Conklin or any of his men to challenge him. None chose to do so. Conklin and some of his "business partners" left the territory as ordered, leaving the gold dust counterfeiting operation with no manager. With Conklin's departure, economic stability was restored to the region.[72]

McConnell had bested the Pickett Corral Gang yet again. However, this wouldn't be the last faceoff between the gang and the vigilance group they'd inadvertently been responsible for founding.

THE SHERIFF AND THE VIGILANTE

Not long after McConnell's showdown with the Pickett Corral Gang, Ada County was created by the territorial legislature. Partitioned off Boise County, Ada County, at that time, included most of present-day Payette, Gem, and Canyon Counties. An area that large certainly needed a lawman to help keep order.

David C. Updyke was a relative newcomer to the Boise Basin. He spent some time in California as a stage driver, had traveled north to British Columbia for a while, and then worked his way back down and landed in Warren, Idaho, a gold mining camp in a remote part of present-day Idaho County, in 1863. Updyke stayed in Warren long enough to earn a reputation as a courageous "Indian fighter," having joined an "expedition to punish marauding Indians" in Central Idaho's gold country. In 1864, though, he was in Boise, bringing his notoriety as a leader with him. Updyke opened a livery stable on Main between Seventh and Eighth Streets in Boise—the stable where McConnell had found his wayward horse—and made connections throughout the Boise Valley. When the newly formed Ada County opened the elections for sheriff, Updyke was a natural choice to run.[73]

Election Day, March 6, 1865, "passed off very quietly there being but one shooting match, and but one or two fist fights."[74] Updyke won the contest for sheriff and tax collector handily, earning more than twice the votes of his two opponents. Despite Updyke's popularity, or perhaps because of it, whispers abounded about his activities in the Treasure Valley prior to running for sheriff. Updyke, some said, was a swindler and cheat. Others claimed that he consorted with murderers and horse thieves. Many suggested that Updyke was not only a member of the notorious Pickett Corral Gang but also one of its leaders. Most damning, though, was a whispered claim that he'd been involved in the 1864 Overland Stage robbery that had injured William Parks.[75]

Updyke's reign as sheriff turned out to be short-lived. In September 1865, just six months after taking office, Updyke faced criminal charges. He was accused of two crimes: letting a suspected murderer walk free and failing to turn in collected tax monies to the county treasurer. Two separate complaints against him had been made related to revenue laws. Updyke had been "unlawfully and feloniously receiving, transferring, and disposing of certain evidences of the indebtedness of Ada County, known as county warrants or orders by a county officer, charged with the collection of the county revenue" and had "refused and neglected to pay over to the treasurer of Ada county a large sum of money, to-wit: one thousand dollars and

David Updyke was a popular figure in Boise. Before, during, and after his embattled stint as Ada County's first sheriff, Updyke owned a livery stable on Main Street. This photo shows Boise's Main Street in 1866. *P73, "Boise Streets—Main, 1866," Idaho State Archives.*

upwards."[76] Updyke, the warrants indicated, had not only neglected to collect taxes from all indebted parties but had also pocketed much of what he collected for himself and, quite possibly, for his criminal friends. The charges also made the whispers about Updyke's involvement with the Pickett Corral Gang and the Overland Stage robbery a bit louder. Now that there were charges for crimes that could be proven, the people of Boise wondered if perhaps those old rumors might have some truth to them.

In response to the warrants, Updyke turned in the outstanding payments to the county treasurer before his trial began. That he hadn't handed over the money earlier, his friends said, was "an oversight." Updyke was "a simple good natured fellow not up to proper bookkeeping."[77] Similarly, a writer with the *Idaho Statesman* claimed that "there were circumstances that made the neglect more excusable than criminal."[78] The charge for keeping county funds was dropped. The other charges, however, stood, and Updyke resigned his position as sheriff on October 5, 1865. The public fervor and uproar over the matter quickly came to an end.

Despite this episode of public corruption, Updyke's connections and personable nature ensured that his popularity in Boise was undiminished. Most members of the public seemed to forget, if not forgive, Updyke's criminal missteps as sheriff and his possible gang involvement. Updyke remained in Boise and returned to running his livery stable. When men were called to volunteer for an excursion against the Paiutes in the Boise, Payette, and Snake River Valleys in February 1866, the former sheriff was quick to volunteer.* The Ada County Volunteers, as they voted to call themselves, selected Updyke as their captain, and he helped whittle the group to about twenty-five men. Later, rumors swirled that many of them were "the daily bar, gambling house, saloon, and pool room habituates" and, possibly, members of Updyke's rumored "gang of cutthroats," the Pickett Corral Gang.[79] Despite the questionable makeup of the group, the residents of the Boise Basin sent the company off with arms and equipment worth about $3,000 (about $53,000 in today's money). The expedition set off to "punish the murdering, thieving Piutes [*sic*]."[80]

The Ada County Volunteers returned to Boise just over three weeks later. They'd traveled east down the Snake River to Bruneau and then turned back westward toward what is now the Oregon border. There the men camped along the Snake in an area they cleared of sagebrush. The Paiutes were nowhere to be found. Upon returning to Boise, Updyke reported that the Paiutes "had become aware of his fighting army's presence, capabilities, and intentions" and in doing so had "panicked in fearful rout all the way out of the entire Idaho territory on into Nevada."[81] According to Updyke's description of events, the company had looked so courageous, poised, and dangerous in their marching and drilling that the Paiutes had fled rather than risk provocation.

In truth, though, the Ada County Volunteers had spent most of their time in the camp on the banks of the Snake River gambling and sporting. They'd constructed a rough racetrack in the cleared area and spent the days racing their horses and placing bets on the riders and animals. The group returned to Boise after they grew tired of "these strenuous war practices."[82]

The people of Boise were none the wiser, though. The Paiutes were no longer causing issues for the valleys' settlers, so the Volunteers' objective had been accomplished. The whole matter may have been forgotten except that the Ada County Volunteers had not kept their activities to simply racing the horses already in their possession. A farmer accused one of the returning expedition members of stealing one of his horses, and the matter quickly went to trial. The Ada County Volunteers all testified on behalf of their

---

* One *Statesman* writer referred to the tribes of southern Idaho as "red demons." Modern readers, I hope, will recognize that the white reports of "murdering" and "thieving" were either greatly exaggerated or acts committed in self-defense and survival. Perhaps a combination of both of those options is closer to the truth. It is vital to recognize that directing accusations of murder and theft solely at Native Americans is an omission of facts and a grave mistruth.

own member, except one—an eighteen-year-old named Rueben Raymond, who spilled the truth about the company's activities while on their mission.[83]

Despite the young man's testimony, which matched the farmer's story, the judge ruled against the farmer. Immediately after the trial, the crowd spilled into the streets, and the Ada County Volunteers surrounded Raymond, pushing and shoving the boy. When Raymond drew his revolver in self-defense, a man named John Clark, an associate of Updyke's and another member of the Ada County Volunteers, also drew. The two faced each other, guns drawn. Clark goaded Raymond to shoot, but the younger man refused. "I don't want to shoot," he said. "I'll give you the first shot."[84]

Clark didn't need any more prompting. His revolver clicked once and then again. The third time, he took "deliberate aim" and shot Raymond in the stomach. Raymond, witnesses said, "did not attempt to shoot at all." Raymond lived through the rest of the afternoon, certainly in excruciating pain and wavering in and out of consciousness. He died that evening.[85]

Clark claimed self-defense. Raymond, he argued, had drawn on him first. In most circumstances in the Old West, this defense may have been valid. However, upon learning the truth of the Ada County Volunteers' full activities, compounded with the witness testimony and outrage of the murder of a teen boy, the people of Boise refused to allow the matter to drop. Clark was taken into custody. Boise's residents also knew that Clark had influential friends, including former sheriff Dave Updyke. There was never a guarantee of conviction for Clark's crime in Idaho Territory.

On the night of April 5, 1866, between fifteen and twenty men forcibly removed John Clark from his cell in the Boise jail. By the time the overpowered guards were able to call for help, Clark and his captors had disappeared into the darkness. Nothing seemed amiss until the next morning, when word spread that a body was hanging from a makeshift gallows on the present-day grounds of the Idaho State Capitol. A note was pinned to John Clark's body:

> *Justice has now commenced her righteous work….Forbearance has at least ceased to be a virtue, and an outraged community has most solemnly resolved on SELF PROTECTION.*
>
> *Let this man's fate be a terrible warning to all his kind, for the argus eye of Justice is no more sure to see than her arm wil [sic] be certain to strike.*
>
> *The soil of this beautiful valley shall no longer be desecrated by the presence of THIEVES and ASSASSINS. This fatal example has no terror for the innocent, but let the guilty beware, and not delay too long, and take warning.*

XXX

The vigilantes had ensured that John Clark faced justice.

"This gentle reminder," one historian noted, "caused quite a disturbance among the sporting set in Boise. In fact, the population of the town decreased immediately." The corrupt and criminal of Boise had been warned, and many, apparently, took that warning to heart.[86]

Former sheriff Updyke took the message seriously. Within days, he'd sold his livery stable and other holdings for below market value, making his plans to depart town public knowledge. Before he left, though, Updyke "was most ferocious in his threats against several citizens, whom he charged with having a hand in the execution [of Clark]." He would return to Boise, he claimed, and when he did, those responsible would pay for their crime.[87] On April 12, 1866, he left Boise on horseback with $3,000 in his pockets. He did not make it very far.[88]

Updyke's body was found hanging from the rafter of a barn thirty miles northeast of Boise on the Rocky Bar road. His pockets were empty, and attached to his corpse was a note reading, "Dave Updyke, the aider of murderers, and horse thieves. XXX." Just a few miles farther down the road hung the body one of Updyke's associates. This body bore a similar note: "Jake Dixon, horse thief and gold counterfeiter." Updyke and Dixon had left town together and, in the process, been caught by vigilantes at the same time. Three days later, Boise residents found a note tacked to the wall of Updyke's former stable.

Dave Updyke
Accessory after the fact to the Portneuf stage robbery.
Accessory and accomplice to the robbery of the stage near Boise City.
Chief conspirator in burning property on the Overland stage route.
Guilty of aiding and assisting West Jenkins the murderer, and other criminals to escape while you were sheriff of Ada County.
Threatening the lives and property of an already outraged, suffering community.
Justice has overtaken you.

X.X.X.

Jake Dixon
Horse thief, counterfeiter, and road agent generally.
A dupe and tool of Dave Updyke.

X.X.X.[89]

Updyke's murderers claimed that he was responsible for several instances of robbery and property destruction along the Portneuf and Overland Stage routes. This photo shows the Overland Stage outside Boise in the late 1800s. *P658, "Stage Coaches—Overland Stage," Idaho State Archives.*

The vigilantes had decided that all the rumors about Updyke's questionable dealings were true and that since the law had failed to hold him accountable, they would ensure that justice would be done.

Updyke's murder spread "great excitement throughout the Basin," and his remaining associates "threaten[ed] to retaliate."[90] Many expected the news coming out of Boise in the weeks following Updyke's death would be filled with more murder and hangings, perhaps of innocent men. "It is an easy matter to strangle the best man in the community and pin a paper on the dead body accusing him of the worst of crimes," an *Idaho World* writer stated in a report on Updyke's death. Some claimed that the murder of Updyke, a Democrat, was part of a larger plot to seat Republicans in the upcoming elections. By "hanging some of the workers whom they fear, and frightening the balance into meekness," the plotters would "carry matters their own way at the polls."[91]

This was not a popular opinion, though. Most early Idahoans, while not condoning vigilantism, understood the purpose that it served. In April 1866, just days after Updyke's death, the *Idaho Statesman* noted:

For something more than two years this Territory has been ridden and ruled by both organized and unorganized bands of men, who have made highway and private robbery, burglary and murder...their profession.... And when there was a faithful officer to take the track of an offender, he soon found his prey so well guarded by confederates that capture was all but an impossibility....The law seemed to present no check to whatever outrages the villains that habitually prey upon society chose to commit.[92]

Without the vigilance committees and men like William McConnell, the writer argued, lawlessness would continue to plague the territory, undermining any attempts at governance and civil society. Idaho Territory needed vigilante justice. David Updyke's reign as sheriff of Ada County, however brief, illustrated that "if the law becomes the secret servant of the criminal, maybe there is little choice other than Vigilantism."[93]

William McConnell, arguably one of the most prominent vigilantes in southern Idaho, with influence stretching from Walla Walla to Montana, went on to have a long and illustrious career in public service in Idaho. Shortly after his activities with the vigilance committees of the Payette Valley and Boise Basin, McConnell married and relocated to Oregon, but he moved back to Idaho in 1884, settling in Moscow and running a mercantile business. In 1890, he sat on the Idaho Constitutional Convention and was elected to the U.S. Senate, where he served for a year. McConnell was elected Idaho's governor in 1892, a position he held until 1897. Governor McConnell made no apologies for his earlier involvement with the vigilantes. The vigilantes had acted, he simply said, because "no effort was being made by those whose duties it was to enforce the law."[94]

Vigilante justice in the Boise Basin didn't come to an end following Updyke's murder in 1866. One historian estimates that between 1860 and 1870, vigilantes in Idaho and Montana hanged nearly two hundred "unsavory individuals."[95] By the turn of the twentieth century, though, the papers were reporting fewer and fewer instances of this form of "Western Justice." However, that didn't mean corruption and criminality in Idaho's capital city came to an end. The City of Trees' largest scandals were yet to come.

Part II

"A NECESSARY EVIL"

Prostitution in Early Boise

"The Dubious, Disjointed Tale of a Precocious Young Prostitute"

In late July 1892, sixteen-year-old Ella Benham sought an audience with Boise police chief Nicholson. Her husband, young Mrs. Benham claimed, had "harshly chided her," and she sought protection from his temper.[96] Mr. Benham, though, pleaded his own case. He'd chastised his wife, yes, but with good cause. Young Ella Benham, he claimed, had been lured into prostitution.[97]

The Benhams had married when Ella was merely fourteen. Mrs. Benham was, according to her husband, a modest girl with "no knowledge of the vice or immorality of this wicked world."[98] That was, of course, until she met two women, identified by the *Idaho Statesman* as Mrs. Ramsey and Ms. Larkins, who persuaded her to forsake her husband and work in Larkins's brothel. His wife, Benham claimed, not only refused his entreaties to return home but also had admitted to him that she'd spent the night with a man in exchange for money while at Ms. Larkins' establishment. This unfortunate series of events had Mr. Benham "very much worked up."[99]

Ramsey and Larkins were arrested and brought to trial. Larkins, a brothel owner, readily admitted that she employed Mrs. Benham. Ramsey, a dressmaker, clarified that the young woman worked at Larkins's house during the day and slept at her home at night. Mrs. Benham's job, Ramsey clarified, was not to entertain men. Mr. Benham, she continued, abused his young wife, forcing her to "live in a dirty barn" and neglecting to supply her with clean clothing. She and Larkins had not induced Mrs. Benham "to enter upon a life of shame," but rather had protected her from the violent and neglectful impulses of her older, abusive husband.[100]

The Benham affair was not confined to courtroom spectacle. The conflict spilled out into Boise's streets. As the first day of the trial ended, friends of the accused followed Mr. Benham from the courthouse. According to an observer, the defendants' supporters—a Mr. and Mrs. Gardner and their eighteen-year-old daughter, reportedly a friend of Mrs. Benham—matched Ramsey and Larkins "in appearance and character." No further details were given, but the writer's tone made it apparent that most of Boise viewed the women and the Gardners as a rough, unrespectable lot a class below the hardworking and decent Benham. As the crowd made their way down Sixth Street from Jefferson toward Main, the Gardners hurled insults across the road at Benham. He responded in kind and, eventually, "goaded into a desperation," called young Miss Gardner a "vicious woman."[101]

Mrs. Gardner pulled away from her husband, dashed at Benham and hit him in the face. "You'll call my daughter a b----, will you?" she shrieked.[102]

Benham drew back far enough to land a swift, hard kick to Mrs. Gardner's stomach. The woman let out a great gasp, and the street devolved into chaos. Miss Gardner ran across the street to her mother's aid. She took a quick hit to the mouth but quickly recovered and "was full of fight" again. Benham, outnumbered, pulled a folding knife from his pocket, and the Gardner women retreated slightly. Mr. Gardner, "who did not appear half as much a man as his wife," the observer noted, muttered, "I'll cut his head off in 15 minutes. I'll cut his head off sure." His wife's "sharp and not overly clean tongue" continued to heap abuse on Benham. Benham, though, according to the witness, "was pure grit and not overawed by their numbers."[103] His rusty blade kept the Gardners at bay, but they continued to follow him down Sixth Street, uttering threats along the way.

Finally, the disagreeable group arrived at Mrs. Ramsey's door. The Gardners' threats and jeers grew louder.

"Oh-h-h-h, you dirty sucker!" Miss Gardner shrieked.

"If he'll come into the alley I'll lick him in less than no time!" Mrs. Gardner cried.

"Let me get a gun! Hold me! Let me get a pistol! I'll bag him before morning!" Mr. Gardner rumbled.[104]

Benham kept moving down the street until he was out of sight and earshot. He kept himself armed throughout the night, though, as he'd been advised that he may have "two or three cowardly men as well as several Amazonian women to deal with."[105]

The court of public opinion was clearly against the defendants. The evidence presented thus far, along with the behavior of their acquaintances, "placed the Ramsay and Larkins women in a bad light." Benham, meanwhile—"a hard working man" who "owned the house in which he lived"—had "honest" people give testimony on his behalf. A Mrs. Chartier swore that she heard Mrs. Benham tell Mr. Benham that "the defendants had promised her both money and clothes if she would come and live with them." A Mr. Carl testified that he'd visited Ramsey's home a number of times and that it was, indeed, "one of bad repute."[106] Two men claimed that Larkins's "general reputation…was bad," and another reported that two women, whose names he could not recall, had inquired about renting his hotel in South Boise for the purpose of converting it to a "'fashionable' bawdy house."[107]

But no one had heard from Ella Benham yet. The girl took the stand on August 24 under the watchful eye of an officer placed in the courtroom "to prevent, if possible, any repetition of the free-for-all fight" between Mr. Benham and the Gardners the day before. An observer noted that Mrs. Benham's testimony was "rambling" and "disconnected," her sentences "short and crabbed." Her story, though, had everyone's attention. "I left my husband's on July 20th because he whipped me," the young woman stated matter-of-factly. "He was jealous of me and said the defendants were not fit persons to associate with.…All his testimony is absolutely false."[108]

Mr. Benham's behavior was not a one-time occurrence. Ella's husband regularly beat her with his fists, often in the face, and he once hit her with a garden hoe. When asked about her association with Ramsey and Larkins, Ella testified that she'd worked for Larkins for two weeks but never stayed in the house after dark. She'd become friends with Ramsey shortly after moving to Boise a year and a half earlier.[109]

A day later, the case was dismissed. The prosecution's flimsy witness testimony had failed to provide enough evidence to justify holding Ramsey and Larkins, and the women were set free. Before a week was up, "the notorious Mrs. Benham" was on a train east to her father's home.[110]

No evidence or direct testimony could prove that Mrs. Ramsey or Ms. Larkins were prostitutes or "enticed Mr. Benham's 16-year-old wife into a house of prostitution."[111] Yet Mr. Benham's accusation—meant to keep his wife, deflect attention from his terrible treatment of her or both—upended the women's lives. Whispers certainly continued to swirl about the two

Trials like those of Mrs. Ramsey and Ms. Larkins were held in the first Ada County Courthouse, pictured here circa 1900. *P1969-4-23, "Boise Public Buildings—Courthouse," Idaho State Archives.*

women long after Ella Benham had escaped Boise and her husband's rough treatment.

Unfortunately, the demonizing of women, especially those who were poor or lived on the outskirts of "polite" society, was not uncommon. In 1898, fourteen-year-old Emma Anderson accused G.T. Anderson of rape. Emma was "a sort of adopted child" of the seventy-seven-year-old Anderson; his family had taken her in when she was about nine months old. Anderson was convicted of the crime in Blaine County and sent to the penitentiary in Boise. A year later, the state supreme court reversed the decision, ruling that "the testimony was insufficient to support the verdict."[112]

The testimony in question came from the victim: young Emma Anderson. Her story was "uncorroborated" with facts or the testimony of other witnesses. Most damning of all, though, the court found flaws in Emma's character. "There was ample evidence to show the girl was loose," and "she did not tell of the offense until long after its commission." Even more, the girl was known, the court claimed, to be "a prostitute...whose reputation for truth and veracity is entirely impeached."[113]

Anderson, meanwhile, was a simple, honest man with an "unblemished" reputation. Emma took advantage of his "charity," to which "she is indebted for her very existence." Considering all this, the court refused to uphold the seven-year sentence, especially considering that its length and Anderson's age most likely meant life in prison. It overturned the conviction, freeing the defendant whom it believed had been convicted "upon the dubious, disjointed tale of a precocious young prostitute."[114]

Emma Anderson, Ella Benham, Mrs. Ramsey, Ms. Larkins and countless other women in the nineteenth and early twentieth centuries—indeed, throughout history—who were unmarried, lived alone, supported themselves, or associated with the "wrong" sorts of people dodged whispers and accusations of immorality. Although "adultery, fornication nor prostitution" were "not actionable *per se* under the statutes of Idaho," the accusation was enough to destroy a woman's life.[115] Many times, those women's only "crimes" were poverty and a failure to comply with social norms, two characteristics that were certainly not mutually exclusive.*

In the early nineteenth century, the Western world operated on the idea that society was made of two spheres: the public and the private. Men ran the public sphere: politics, economics, medicine, and education. The private sphere was the domain of women. This idea that a woman's responsibilities lie solely with her home and children, called the "cult of true womanhood" or "cult of domesticity," "tied a woman's virtue to her piety, submissiveness, and domesticity."[116] Women were expected to be completely dependent, both economically and socially, on the men in their lives. Unmarried, childless women—even those with independent incomes, homes, and stable personal lives—fell far outside this norm.

Prostitutes were an even further outlier in Victorian society.† As members of the public sphere, Boise's prostitutes lived in stark contrast to "proper Victorian women," but they were an important thread in the city's social fabric. Victorian belief held that the "public woman" saved the woman in the private sphere from "male lust and pregnancy from marriage until death" by providing another outlet for his sexual energy. She also provided a

---

* In 1895, the Idaho Supreme Court awarded Jennie Douglas $1,650. She had sued her husband, Thomas Douglas, for $5,000 for slander after he publicly declared her an "unchaste woman" and accused her of sexual relations with his brother prior to their marriage. Mrs. Douglas won because, under Idaho law, prostitution, adultery and fornication—of which she'd been accused—were not punishable offenses at the time. Though materially on the positive end of the ruling, Mrs. Thomas undoubtedly suffered social consequences, the likes of which $1,650 may have done little to assuage.
† The term *prostitute* has fallen out of favor in recent years. Today, the term *sex worker* is preferred to describe those who engage in sex work. Although "language is an important battle ground in the fight for social equality," the term *prostitute* will be used in this work, as it was the common terminology at the time in question.

valuable lesson in what might befall a woman should she fail to follow "the dictates of the True Womanhood." Additionally, early Boise's sex workers played a vital role in the city's economy. Their rents and business kept a number of Boise landlords and businessmen wealthy, and for several years, the regulatory fines and fees prostitutes were charged added to the budget of the city's police department.[117]

Prostitution's public reception changed over Boise's first half century. From open, yet perhaps unspoken, acceptance to outright hostility, prostitution was always along the fringes of Boise society—an area often filled with danger, scandal and crime for everyone—men and women alike—associated with the "disorderly" and "debauched" part of the public sphere.

A CRUSADE AGAINST "HAUNTS OF DISSIPATION AND DEBAUCHERY"

Arguably, most of Boise's "public women" did not freely choose their trade, but rather sold sex as a matter of survival. Due to unfortunate life circumstances, they found themselves with few other options for support and subsistence. Many young women found themselves in Boise's "bawdy houses" after the death of a parent or spouse. Others had been abandoned by wayward husbands and had no way to feed and clothe themselves and their children. Some, like Ella Benham, were fleeing abuse. Many women used sex work to supplement the meager income earned as a laundress, seamstress, or housekeeper. Twenty-four-year-old Maria Kennedy was the mother of three children under the age of three. Mary Webber was thirty and had five children under seven. Elicia Hennessy, by age thirty-two, had six children. The oldest was thirteen, the youngest nine months. Jane Lyons, twenty-five, was single and childless. These women were Fort Boise's only female residents. Their work as laundresses (Lyons had no officially recorded job) brought them each less than $20 per month (less than $600 today), so it's not far-fetched to assume that they all engaged in sex work in order to support themselves and their children.[118]

Assuming that all of Boise's prostitutes were unfortunate victims of circumstance living helpless lives would be a disservice, though. Some were career sex workers; they moved around the west from city to city, following economic booms and busts. Others chose to stay in the profession even after marrying or accumulating enough wealth to retire. They enjoyed the money and status their business garnered. Eleanor Dumont, the famed "Madame Moustache," briefly brought her business to Boise in 1863 during travels around the West that included the gold fields of California and Nevada; the mining city of Butte, Montana; and other frontier boomtowns. Isabel Roques made a "fortune" selling sex in the Boise Basin and moved her practice to Boise, where she owned a house in the middle of the city's red-light district.[119] Women like Madame Moustache and Isabel Roques were happy to live their lives unconstrained by the rules of contemporary feminism and the Cult of True Womanhood. Like today's modern career-minded women, Boise's early prostitutes had varied reasons and motivations for working and for their chosen line of work.

Boise's first twenty-five years were marked by a period of uneasy acceptance of prostitution. Early Boise was a prototypical rough and wild frontier town. Boise's first prostitutes settled near Fort Boise, at the intersection of Garrison and Idaho Streets, then one of the most well-traveled spots in town. The women provided a welcome distraction for soldiers stationed at the fort and travelers on their way to and from the gold fields of the Boise Basin. Women opened parlor houses and rented rooms wherever they knew business would be good—in or near saloons, gambling parlors, or distilleries. That is not to say that life was easy for Boise's earliest prostitutes. The women often faced

An early view of Fort Boise. Many of the city's earliest sex workers lived around Fort Boise, which was then one of the busiest areas of the city. *P1977-180-2c, "Boise Military Post—Fort Boise," Idaho State Archives.*

violence, derision, and scorn that many found unbearable. When Elizabeth Tummette's husband left her in 1866, she had no option but to find work, including sex work, in a saloon. Tummette, abandoned and destitute, swallowed oxalic acid and died by suicide.[120]

Although many experienced personal hardships and social isolation, most of Boise's earliest prostitutes were able to live their lives free of legal consequences. Idaho Territory's laws gave Boise officials the authority to regulate prostitution and "houses of ill-fame," but for a time the city took a hands-off approach. The women didn't lose any of their money to fines and fees, and many were probably able to make a fairly successful, if not profitable, living. At least some of Boise's prostitutes during the city's first twenty-five years owned their own property. The overwhelmingly male populace, while certainly not always respectful of the city's prostitutes, well understood that these women and the services they provided were vital for "peace" in the rough Wild West town.[121]

By the 1880s, though, Boise had grown from a wild frontier outpost into a modern Victorian city. The population swelled and business changed. Merchants and professionals of all trades—law, education, medicine, commerce, and more—lived with their families in residential neighborhoods and worked in the offices that were built in, around, and over the remains of the city's early storefronts and saloons. Boise lost its rough-and-tumble atmosphere. Vigilante justice became less common as the city's infrastructure grew to support more formal law enforcement. Boise had become a respectable, family-friendly city, soon to become the capital of the new state of Idaho.

Across the nation, the late nineteenth century was marked with social reform movements. Reform societies such as the Woman's Christian Temperance Union (WCTU) came to prominence. The women of the WCTU were on a mission to protect their homes from dangerous outside influences. This included, of course, prostitution. Backed by the clergy, these movements sought to protect families and children from the "haunts of dissipation and debauchery." Victorian women, in an effort to protect the sanctity of their private spheres, took an active interest in improving the public sphere. Women reformers were often sympathetic to the plights of prostitutes. They viewed "public women" as poor, uneducated victims, "lured into immorality by licentious men." Members of the all-male clergy saw the situation differently. Prostitutes were "vile temptresses," responsible for luring "innocent young men…into their evil dens." Regardless of their contrasting views on prostitutes, female reformers and the clergy had the same goal: to rid their city of "dens of prostitution."[122]

Despite their differences in opinion on the whys and whats of prostitution in general, the reformers and the clergy both agreed that something needed to be done to clean up the city. In the mid-1890s, the city welcomed evangelist Charles Crittenton, who had started homes for "fallen women" in several larger American cities. In the Florence Crittenton homes, named in memory of Crittenton's deceased four-year-old daughter, women were taken from their lives on the streets and given the skills and knowledge necessary to lead lives of "purity…domesticity and submission to men." The home gave "fallen women" the opportunity to become "True Women." Rather than a refuge to help reform prostitutes, though, Boise's Crittenton Home quickly became a home strictly for unwed mothers. While many of Boise's female sex workers certainly had children, it's likely that they were not the Crittenton Home's primary recruits. The city of Boise took a different approach to prostitution. Rather than supporting reform, authorities chose to stick with enforcement and strict regulation.[123]

In 1889, Boise waged its first real "war on sin." Reformers launched a campaign urging city officials to follow the statutes against brothels laid out by the Idaho Territory legislature in 1877. Boise authorities had, for far too long, reformers argued, ignored the laws that could "assert American loyalty to home and family and children." City officials responded by arresting several men and women accused of owning and operating houses of prostitution. The *Idaho Statesman* joined the campaign, printing several letters and editorials throughout the trial encouraging the jury to convict the accused. According to the *Statesman*, several of the accused left town. Those who remained were put on trial, found guilty, fined, and admonished "to return to the paths of rectitude." The 1889 trial was the beginning of formal regulation of Boise's prostitutes. Following the decision, "the city council passed an ordinance prohibiting the operation of bawdy houses, or houses of ill fame within thirteen blocks of a public school." The ordinance applied to anyone owning or renting any room or apartment on the property.[124]

The ruling and new ordinance were certainly a victory for the reformers, but far from their ultimate desired outcome. Though regulated, prostitution was still allowed to exist in their city. Many people, though, realized that the regulation of prostitution had many benefits, though none of them for the women engaged in sex work. Parents, especially concerned mothers, believed that prostitution provided an outlet for lusty young men, thereby protecting their daughters from unwanted sexual attention. The clergy also claimed that members of Boise's demimonde could be used "as an example to keep good women on the narrow path of purity and virtue."* In these cases, prostitution was "a necessary evil."[125] City officials came to realize that the fines and fees gathered not only benefited the city's coffers but also helped line individual pockets of unscrupulous bribe-takers. Several Boise property owners set to work creating "a Whitechapel in their own town."[126] Idaho Street, particularly the alley between Idaho and Main, from Sixth to Ninth Streets, was the location chosen for Boise's Whitechapel.† If prostitution could not be abolished, it would certainly be contained, and this was of much greater benefit to many city authorities and property owners. Establishing a regulated, specific area for houses of prostitution made many landlords very rich.

Ellen Bush was the daughter of *Idaho Statesman* editor Judge Milton Kelly, a "prominent citizen" of Boise. Her mother, Lois Kelly, was an active women's rights reformer. Bush herself was a well-educated college graduate, had married a successful businessman and held several valuable Boise properties. She'd inherited properties from both her deceased husband and her father. One of her properties, on the 600 block of Main Street in the heart of the red-light district, had four cribs—tiny, shack-like rooms used for prostitution—built behind it. She also owned a female boardinghouse—a popular euphemism for brothel—on the corner of Seventh and Idaho. A crib sat next to the boardinghouse, and another of Bush's properties sat nearby; its entrance faced the Idaho Street alley. Bush, it seems, rented her properties to madams and sex workers and made a very good living doing so. The Bush Mansion still stands on Franklin Street behind Boise High School.[127]

Ellen Bush, though, is an anomaly. Most of the landlords within Boise's red-light district were male. Two of the most notorious were Davis Levy and John Broadbent. Broadbent's properties included a parlor house with several rooms to rent (only accessible from the alley) and a female boardinghouse. Several cribs sat in the alley in proximity to these buildings. Broadbent's property holdings in downtown Boise were enormous. Upon his death in 1922, his estate was worth $2.5 million.[128]

Davis Levy, though, was Boise's most notorious red-light district landlord. A Prussian immigrant, Levy arrived in Boise in 1867 and opened a bakery

---

* *Demimonde* is French for "half-world." The term was first used in a play by Alexandre Dumas, author of such works as *The Count of Monte Cristo* and *The Three Musketeers*. Demimonde came to refer to those living on the fringes of respected society or individuals, particularly women, of what was considered "ambiguous moral character."

† Whitechapel is a neighborhood in East London, most well known for its overcrowding and poverty in the nineteenth century. The neighborhood is also notorious as the haunt of the infamous serial killer Jack the Ripper, who preyed on Whitechapel sex workers.

Boise's City Hall, on the corner of Eighth and Idaho Streets, circa 1905. City hall's location puts it right next to the red-light district. The present-day location of city hall, on Capital (previously Seventh Street) between Idaho and Main, sits within the boundaries of the old red-light district. *P1984-11-12, "Boise Public Buildings—City Hall circa 1905," Idaho State Archives.*

at Sixth and Main. He was incredibly successful and eventually opened a lodging house above the bakery and began investing in real estate. Before long, Levy owned half of Main Street's north block, the present-day location of Boise City Hall.[129]

Baking and real estate were far from Levy's only business pursuits. The 1870 census labeled Levy as a "huckster," a nineteenth-century term for entrepreneur. Levy seized every possible opportunity he saw to make money. An 1872 *Idaho Statesman* piece noted that Levy not only ran the bakery but also owned "a grocery and a saloon, a lunch house, and candy shop…a vegetable depot…a commission business," and soon he "expected to have a tannery and sawmill connected with his establishment." Levy was on his way to becoming one of Boise's most successful businessmen and community members.[130]

By the early 1890s, though, following this series of misfortunes, Levy's business interests in Boise had taken a turn. The city directories from 1890 to the turn of the century didn't list Levy as a baker, but rather a "saloon keeper, a purveyor of general merchandise, a capitalist, and a real-estate speculator." Most of these broad and general terms can be used as "poetic euphemisms" for his most lucrative business: brothel landlord. Already the biggest property owner within what became Boise's Whitechapel, Levy capitalized on the city's decision to move prostitution into the area. He constructed a number of cribs in the alley behind his properties. The alley between Idaho and Main between Sixth and Eighth became known as "Levy's Alley."[131]

Not only did landlords like Levy and Broadbent make a fortune renting their properties to Boise's sex workers and madams, but they also seemed largely immune from any consequences of these activities. In May 1901, both Levy and Broadbent were called into court to answer for charges that they "were permitting houses of ill fame" to operate in their properties. Levy pleaded not guilty. The evidence presented on both sides was based on hearsay and anecdotes used to determine the reputation of the property in question. The mayor, J.H. Richards, was called as a witness and stated that he would follow past precedent "in regard to bawdy houses" and "would not be party to any prosecution of this nature." Richards saw no need for prosecution, as it had never been taken against landlords in the past. Nevertheless, Levy was found guilty and fined forty-four dollars. On appeal, though, a jury reversed the conviction.[132]

Broadbent's trial finally came up about ten months after the initial charge. At that point, Mayor pro tem Henry Parnell wrote a letter to the court. According to Parnell, "The majority of the city council" believed "no further proceedings be had in the case of the State v Broadbent." The county attorney was asked to dismiss the case at the request of the city council. No reason was given. Broadbent and Levy, it seems, both had influence with the people of Boise (evidenced by Levy's jury appeal reversal) and city officials (illustrated by Broadbent's case).[133]

Ellen Bush, interestingly, was never brought up on charges, despite clear evidence that her properties were used for the purposes of prostitution. City officials had no issues with prosecuting women for crimes related to prostitution, so Bush's gender is probably not how she escaped legal trouble. Instead, her social status is the likely reason why her fringe involvement in the sex trade was overlooked. Bush had inherited, it seems, not only her father's and husband's properties but also their standing in Boise society.

Boise's "working women" certainly did not escape the fees, charges, and associated fines that came with the regulation of prostitution. Working within the literal and figurative boundaries established for them, Boise's prostitutes continued to ply their trade in the city. Business within the city's red-light district was its own micro-socioeconomic system. Many of Boise's prostitutes were well known about town. They "were out on the streets by 4 o'clock in the afternoon, dressed in their best clothes," to shop and conduct their personal business. Their work began with the evening. Women would entertain men in saloons, which were often on the first floor of a "bawdy house," and in their private rooms upstairs.[134]

One of these women's biggest expenses was rent. In most cases, the rate was about twenty dollars per week. The rent went either to the property owner or to a madam. The madam, who either rented a house from someone like Davis Levy, John Broadbent, or Ellen Bush or owned her own large parlor house, rented rooms to prostitutes who worked for them. The madams did not engage in sex work themselves, mostly to avoid competition with their workers but also because running the parlor house took the majority of their time. Madams were landlords and bar owners. They mentored the women who worked for them; purchased all the supplies for the house; and hired bartenders, housekeepers, and kitchen staff. They "ran interference with the officers of the law," negotiating fines and fees whenever a slightly unscrupulous officer raided her house, and raised funds for fines and bails when punishment could not be avoided. Madams were business owners with the same concerns other Boise business owners: reputation, client base, and profit margins.[135]

Along with their rent, every member of Boise's demimonde was subject to regular fines by the city police. By 1909, each woman had paid her fines at the police station on the twentieth of each month at 2:00 p.m. The payment allowed her to remain in business for another month without fear of arrest. Additionally, each woman paid $1.50 twice per month for required medical exams. For Boise's working women, these fines and fees were regular costs of doing business.[136]

The prostitutes in parlor houses generally fared better than their counterparts living in the small alleyway cribs. The cribs were miserable, dreary places—a single, cold room with little more than a bed. Women who rented the cribs were sometimes those at the end of their careers. They had reached "the end of the line," so to speak. Others were transient, moving from crib to crib, house to crib, crib to house, and even in and out of Boise. Many were alcoholics or opium addicts. Perhaps their addictions stemmed from their occupation; maybe their occupation grew out of the addiction. A contemporary sex worker explained that "a crib woman" was often trapped in an unhealthy relationship with a man who served, even informally, as her pimp. Perhaps feeling "trapped by her situation," the crib prostitute worked to support not only herself but also her lover, as she feared "the loss of 'the most despicable man.'" Whatever the case,

By 1909, each one of Boise's "working women" showed up at the police station on the twentieth of each month at 2:00 p.m. to pay her monthly fines. The payment allowed her to work for another month without fear of arrest. Pictured are members of the Boise Police Department sometime in the late nineteenth to early twentieth century. *P984-110-10, "Boise Police," Idaho State Archives.*

the women in the cribs generally made only about twenty-five dollars per week. Reselling liquor to generate a bit of extra income was not an uncommon practice among women in cribs.[137]

Women in parlor houses made twice as much as crib prostitutes—at least fifty dollars per week. They did pay the madam room and board and a percentage of their earnings, but they were afforded the protection of the madam, training, and "a sense of community with the other women working in the house."[138] This community was especially important for these women, as they experienced no shortage of violence, public shame, and legal troubles, and their neighborhood—the notorious alley between Idaho and Main—proved dangerous and deadly for many of its inhabitants, regardless of gender or social status.

THE PRIVATE LIVES OF PUBLIC WOMEN

The 1889 trial that signified the start of official regulation of the city's sex trade rested, in part, on one large question: whether a Boise establishment, known as 444, was a brothel. Nettie Bowen was one of Boise's most infamous "courtesans" and widely believed to be 444's keeper. She pleaded not guilty to the charges that she ran a house of ill repute. The prosecution brought forward a number of witnesses—including a city judge, a well-known reverend, law enforcement officers, and several prominent citizens—to help "prove the reputation of '444' was bad." Witnesses testified to issuing Nettie a liquor license for the house. Although they couldn't definitively prove that Nettie owned 444, they swore they had often seen her there, and "she had the reputation of being the mistress of the establishment."* Despite the obvious lack of hard evidence and the "facts" based on community conjecture, Nettie was found guilty of "lewdness and vagrancy" and ordered to pay a fine of $150 (about $4,000 today) and ordered to serve four months in jail. The Idaho Supreme Court later revoked the jail time.[139]

After the 444 trial, Nettie moved down the Treasure Valley to Nampa. Her run-ins with the law, though, did not come to an end. On June 13, 1890, Nettie had a vehement argument with a Mr. Anderson, the owner of a Nampa restaurant Nettie was visiting. While it's unknown what the argument was about, it culminated in Anderson physically removing Nettie from his establishment. "Considerably bruised," perhaps both physically and emotionally, from the encounter, Nettie returned to her rented room. A short while later, though, she stalked back to Anderson's restaurant, this time with a pistol in her hand. Nettie raised her arm, perhaps in pain and shaking with rage, humiliation or a combination of all those, and pulled the trigger. The bullet passed through Anderson's arm and hit the buckle of his suspenders, "thereby Anderson's life was saved."[140]

Nettie turned herself in the next day and pleaded guilty to assault and battery. She paid her $100 fine and was freed; then she immediately sued Anderson for assault. He also quickly pleaded guilty and paid a fine of $50. Nettie's accusation against Anderson and his subsequent guilty plea show

---

* One must wonder how the men called as witnesses were able to argue that 444 was a brothel while also stating under oath that they'd visited many times and still keep their good reputations. Certainly, some law enforcement officers would be permitted to visit the establishment for reasons of enforcement, but what of the reverend and other "prominent citizens of Boise"? Though admitting to repeated visits to a rumored "house of ill-fame," their reputations were not put on trial, but rather used as the prosecution's main weapons, highlighting the hypocrisy that surrounded the city's treatment of suspected prostitutes and women of low social status.

that the events of June 13, 1890, were much more nuanced than the *Statesman* reported. The physical altercation between Nettie and Anderson must have been substantial. Considering the derogatory and dismissive manner the *Statesman* and others generally used when discussing women "of the town" like Nettie, "considerable bruising" was likely not her only injury. However, reports failed to mention Anderson's actions and responsibility in the fray. Likewise, the events that unfolded next—and throughout the remainder of Nettie's life—also illustrate the intense scrutiny, hypocritical treatment by the law and social systems, and violence at the hands of men that Nettie and other women like her endured.[141]

Just three days after the events in Nampa, the district attorney issued a warrant for Nettie's arrest. This action was "the result of a careful investigation" that led him to believe that "a much more serious offense had been committed than that of simple assault and battery." The writer for the *Statesman* concurred, stating that "there is no reason" why Nettie shouldn't be held to account "for the offense now charged."[142] There was no mention of Anderson or his role in the circumstances that led to Nettie's actions on the thirteenth. The judge who heard the case agreed. He believed not only that there was a crime but also "that there was a strong probability that the defendant [Nettie] was the one who committed it." Nettie was held on $1,000 bail until the grand jury could hear her case. For his part, Anderson was held on $500, but only so that he might testify.[143]

While both Nettie and Anderson were held somewhat accountable by the law, the personal fallout they experienced varied greatly. After hearing that she would go before the court charged with assault with intent to murder, Nettie petitioned for a return of the $100 she'd paid for pleading guilty to assault and battery. The fine she'd paid was illegal, Nettie argued, since she was then charged again for the same crime. Her petition was denied. Less than a week later, the house she lived in caught fire. Inspectors believed that the blaze was set intentionally. Fortunately, it had been caught "in time to frustrate the designs of the firebug," and the house sustained very little damage. Just a week and half after the attempted arson, Nettie attempted suicide. "The motive" for her actions, the *Statesman* reported, were unclear. That statement alone illustrates the lack of concern, if not outright disdain, women like Nettie faced in the court of popular opinion. The summer's events had undeniably taken a toll on her.[144]

The *Statesman* never reported the full story of what transpired at Anderson's restaurant in June 1890, but the grand jury ultimately acquitted Nellie of the charge of assault with intent to commit murder. It either agreed that since her guilty plea had been accepted, she couldn't be charged again for the crime, or it believed that her actions were a clear case of self-defense. Perhaps Anderson's role in the events was not nearly as innocuous as reports suggested. Though legally vindicated, Nellie suffered an incredibly high price. She lost money and almost her home and life.[145]

Nettie made her way back to Boise and took up residence on Sixth Street between Main and Idaho. There she was, once again, the topic of newspaper gossip. On November 24, 1891, residents and visitors in the vicinity of Sixth and Idaho were disturbed by a violent commotion. "Pandemonium reigned" as shouts and crashes spilled from a house into the street. Glass shattered when one of the combatants threw a lamp. Neighbors called for the police. The officer who responded to the melee found a man named Jimmy Turner outside the house. Inside, a tearful Nettie Bowen attested through her "swollen nose" that "Turner had 'smashed' her," and "she wanted him arrested 'real bad.'" Turner was immediately arrested, but not before "charming Nettie" was able to land a solid punch to his jaw.[146]

Despite the *Statesman*'s obvious tongue-in-cheek remarks about Nettie's personality, public opinion was more in her favor after this fray than with her dispute with Anderson. Perhaps it's because Boise society held Jimmy Turner in very low regard. Turner was a gambler—"a well-known 'sport'"—and a hard drinker. Turner was convicted of assault, fined twenty dollars, and jailed for five days. At the time of his conviction, Turner had "consumed so much bad whisky" that he was too ill to be held in the county prison. Boise had just as little sympathy, it seems, for Turner than the women of "shady reputation."[147]

Unfortunately, Nettie's run-ins with Turner were not over. Early in the morning of March 28, 1892, the police were called to one of the cribs in the alley between Main, Idaho, Sixth, and Seventh Streets. Inside, they found Nettie and Turner. The former was badly bruised and "severely beaten." The latter was bleeding from wounds in an arm and had a broken knife blade embedded in his leg. The police easily determined how events had transpired and viewed this a clear case of self-defense. Nettie, "the police say…is well behaved when decently treated" and "not at all disposed to be quarrelsome." Jimmy Turner ended up facing charges for the fray. Nettie had him charged with assault and disturbing the peace, but when the time to testify against him came, she was absent. Turner was freed because no one, including Nettie, showed up to testify against him. A number of factors may have kept Nettie from showing in court. Perhaps she feared Turner's retribution. Maybe she preferred to stay away from the eyes of the law as

Pictured is Boise's Main Street between 1896 and 1902. Some of the businesses that lined Main had back entrances leading to the rooms rented by prostitutes. Cribs lined parts of the alley between Idaho and Main between Sixth and Ninth Streets. *P1960-111-2, "Boise Streets—Main between 1890–1902," Idaho State Archives.*

much as possible. Whatever the case, her absence is striking and suggests that although Nettie had the upper hand in this particular affair, she still felt her social situation precarious enough that ensuring justice for Turner was not worth the risk of more public scrutiny. Perhaps she simply felt that she'd done enough by stabbing Turner herself and carrying out her "oft-repeated threat of revenge" for the rough treatment she endured.[148]

Nettie remained a figure in Boise's red-light district and the newspapers for a few more years. Later in 1892, a brothel Nettie reportedly ran was raided, and several women who worked for her were arrested and fined twenty dollars each. In early summer of 1894, she was fined ten dollars and ordered to serve forty days for disorderly conduct for breaking "window lights" in another woman's home. She was released on bail. A year later, she was arrested again, this time for hitting a man "in the head with a water pitcher." The charges were dismissed after enough witnesses testified that she'd acted in self-defense. Then, in July 1896, word came from Silver City that Nettie had died of a morphine overdose. Many believed that Nettie self-medicated with "suicidal intent."[149]

Nettie Bowen's tumultuous and violent life is, unfortunately, only one example of a larger pattern that illustrated life for many women in Boise's red-light district. Public opinion was rarely in their favor. Newspapers and officials treated them with derision. Confrontations between sex workers and their customers were common, and many of them turned violent. The *Statesman* documented several arguments like those Nettie had with Turner and other men. Madams did their best to protect their "girls" from violent customers. In August 1892, a belligerent man tried to break into a brothel in Levi's Alley. The madam met him with shots from a .22-caliber pistol.[150]

Many women also had the same fate as Nettie. In September 1903, young Lela Lewis and her "male companion" said goodnight to Mary Bowen (no relation to Nettie) before the couple and Mary retired to their respective rooms. A few short minutes later, Lela and the man heard someone crying followed by a pistol shot. The man rushed for Mary's door and forced his way into her room. He and Lela found Mary on her bed, "blood pouring from her breast and mouth." The police determined she had put a .45-caliber pistol to her chest and pulled the trigger. Mary and Lela, the *Statesman* reported, had "been quite conspicuous" around town lately. They'd "dressed in flaming red" and "strutted about…attract[ing] considerable attention." Mary's despondency, the paper claimed, was due to the fact her lover had recently left town. The writer seemed unable to comprehend that Mary's lively outings with Lela may have been masking some other unhappiness.[151]

Just a day after Mary's death, Grace Ashton, "a scarlet woman," died at St. Alphonsus hospital. Grace had taken a lethal dose of antiseptic tablets five days earlier. She lived in what must have been agonizing pain as the chemicals in the pills burned through the delicate lining of her stomach. Although she left addresses for her mother in Wyoming and a man in Seattle whom many believed was her husband, Grace's friends paid for her simple funeral.[152]

The ways the *Statesman* reported these incidents exemplified and shaped how the rest of Boise viewed the women who lived and worked in the alley between Idaho, Main, Sixth, and Seventh Streets. The notice of Nettie Bowen's death referred to her as "a notorious courtesan." The article reporting the madam's shooting of a male intruder bore a headline reading "A Notorious Rounder Foiled by an Enraged Female." Although gamblers weren't popular figures with Boise's polite society, the headline's characterization of the madam conjures the image of a bad-tempered, shrewish woman, not one of a strong woman acting in protection of herself, her home and those she is responsible for. The details surrounding Mary Bowen's death were reported in full, gory detail. Mary was described as both "wretched" and "melancholy," and her entire life, not just her death, was investigated. Grace Ashton was described not only as a "scarlet woman" but also as an "inmate" of a lodging house. Had these women been residents of one of the city's more "proper" neighborhoods, living their lives safely within the private sphere, certainly the headlines and stories would have read differently.[153]

Even women who had left the sex trade were subject to this same scorn and scrutiny. In July 1904, William Biggerstaff Jr. married a former sex worker named Marie over the objections of his father, the justice of the peace. The younger Biggerstaff's union was a short one. In October 1904, William placed a series of ads in the *Statesman* stating that he would not be held responsible for any debts accrued by his wife. Marie often visited her husband's workplace in an attempt to win him back, but to no avail. On the same day the last advertisement ran, the paper also reported the death of Mrs. William Biggerstaff. The woman had "died in agony…from the effects of poison taken a week ago with suicidal intent." Mrs. Biggerstaff, it seems, had taken poison on one of her unsuccessful visits to her husband's place of employment—on the same day the first ad ran in the paper. Before her marriage, the young woman, the *Statesman* read, had "led a fast life" as a resident of one of Boise's "disreputable house[s]." Her father, a prosperous clothier in Portland, refused to pay for her burial. That task was left to "unknown friends." Whether or not Marie Biggerstaff's past was the cause of her marital problems is unknown. The *Statesman*, though, thought it important to report her time as a sex worker, a detail that certainly negatively colored the rest of the woman's life for all who read the report.[154]

As evidenced by the court cases of Davis Levy, John Broadbent, and others, justice for the men involved in Boise's sex trade was often lacking. Many of the men accused of running brothels, "enticing" young women into "houses of ill fame for the purposes of prostitution," or profiting from the trade in other ways, escaped without consequences. Others, though, especially those without social connections or deep pockets to bribe officials, did see some form of justice. Anderson, Nettie Bowen's enemy in Nampa, was held to account, at least partially, for his role in their violent altercation. Jimmy Turner faced charges for his part in the fray that led to Nettie stabbing him. Mr. Briggs, Mary Bowen's lover, was called to court, chastised by the judge and charged and fined for "being an inmate of a house of ill repute."[155]

Although Davis Levy was acquitted in a court of law, he was not acquitted in the court of public opinion, and the justice that finally caught up with Levy was far swifter and more brutal than any the justice system could have ordered. Of all sins committed in the red-light district, Davis Levy's story still has a prominent place in Boise lore.

Murder in Levy's Alley

On October 5, 1901, a group of Boise men made a gruesome discovery. A lodger in one of Davis Levy's buildings commented that he hadn't seen the landlord in some time. Two of his acquaintances concurred and commented on an offensive "stench [that] was permeating the block." Concerned for Levy's well-being, they went to the second floor of 612½ Main, where Levy kept his personal rooms. The smell, they realized, was coming from the room next door—a bedroom that Levy rented out to lodgers. The men knocked at the door but were met with silence. The doors and windows were tightly locked. The men called the police, who were able to find keys that opened the door. Inside, the stench was overpowering, and the sight was horrifying. Levy was lying on the bed, a cloud of flies buzzing over him. His hands and feet were tied, and his head was covered with a bloodstained towel and a pillow. Underneath, officers found that Levy's mouth had been stuffed with a piece of cloth. A rope was wrapped tightly around his neck three times, and "blood and gas [were] oozing out of the mouth." The sight, and certainly the smell, "was loathsome in the extreme." Several of the men had to turn away and leave the room.[156]

Upon initial investigation, police noticed signs that indicated Levy hadn't been killed in the lodging room, but rather in the eight-by-ten foot "filthy den" next to it he used as a personal office, kitchen, and bedroom. A half-eaten meal sat on the table. The chair had its back to the door, leading officers to surmise that Levy had been attacked while dining. An autopsy later concluded that Levy had been "sandbagged"—knocked heavily in the back of the head and rendered unconscious. The killer(s) had then dragged him to the next room, where he'd awakened only to be strangled. The room Levy kept for himself, the *Statesman* reported, was "literally covered with grime and filth." Everything "was filthy beyond description, and it is strange how a human being could live in such a place." Word traveled quickly around Boise that "the old miser, who had been such a familiar figure" in town had met a terrible end.[157]

How did Davis Levy, once one of Boise's richest property owners and a well-respected community member, come to live so squalidly and be held in such low regard? Things turned sour for Levy beginning in 1879, when his buildings on Main Street were destroyed by fire. Levy vowed to rebuild bigger and better than ever. "I have started up my bakery," he wrote in a March 1880 ad in the *Statesman*. "I have more experience, and can do the best baking, and don't you forget it," he added, after promising "larger loaves

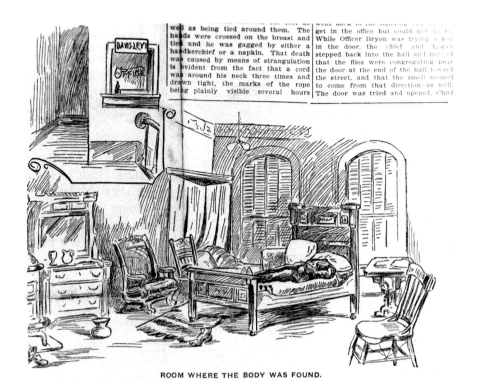

well as being tied around them. The hands were crossed on the breast and tied and he was gagged by either a handkerchief or a napkin. That death was caused by means of strangulation is evident from the fact that a cord was around his neck three times and drawn tight, the marks of the rope being plainly visible several hours

went back to the bathroom ... get in the office but could not ... While Officer Bryon was trying ... in the door, the chief and Logan stepped back into the hall and notified that the flies were congregating near the door at the end of the hall toward the street, and that the smell seemed to come from that direction as well. The door was tried and opened, Chief

ROOM WHERE THE BODY WAS FOUND.

This illustration of the scene of Davis Levy's murder appeared in the *Idaho Statesman* shortly after the crime was committed. *P1973-2-87b, "Davis Levy Murder, Idaho Statesman Drawing," Idaho State Archives.*

at lower prices" than ever seen in the city. Levy's return to the bakery and his other business outlets, though, was soon marred by more trouble. Between 1884 and 1890, Levy was robbed at gunpoint, had eighty dollars stolen by two men who literally held his feet to a fire, was the victim of arson, and was involved in a fight in his saloon with two soldiers who "endeavored to swab out the place of business using the proprietor for a mop." Many of his troubles, though, Levy brought about himself. In July 1882, he was arrested and fined for disturbing the peace. Two years later, he was charged with assault and battery. Both charges stemmed from scrapes he'd had with other men, both of whom were also charged. In one case, Levy was acquitted; the other required payment of a small fine.[158]

With Levy's foray in the 1890s into the business of renting to brothel managers and sex workers, his reputation around town continued to sink. The problems Levy ran into now were nearly entirely of his own making. In December 1891, Levy was arrested for beating one of the women renting a room from him. Not six months later, he was arrested for committing the same crime again. The "brutal act," though, only cost him a thirteen-dollar fine. Levy reportedly visited each of his female lodgers daily at 1:00 p.m. to collect their rent. The price was steep—two dollars per day—and if the women were unable to pay, "he often beat them with his fists."* Levy's "den of horrors" was one of the primary examples cited in the Boise reformers' efforts to end prostitution in the city.[159]

Davis Levy had become "a typical miser," the *Statesman* reported, "greedy, crafty, and cruel."[160] He was loathed and feared. According to local rumor, though, he also had very deep pockets. Police didn't have to look very hard for motive in Levy's murder. An old trunk in his rooms had been wrenched open, its contents pillaged and spilled across the floor. The papers strewn about the room included collectible notes and bank deposits indicating that Levy had a considerable bank account. Beside the body, police found a set of keys, a bracelet, and a leather bag that witnesses say Levy had carried cash in. The bag was empty. Later, appraisers would value his estate at more than $71,000 (nearly $2 million today). Investigators estimated that Levy's killer, or killers, got away with about $500.[161]

With a solid motive established, police set out to find those responsible. The governor put up a $1,000 reward on behalf of the State of Idaho, and Levy's relatives added another $3,000. Suspects, though, were scarce. A thorough search of Levy's room and the rest of the building yielded no clues. All the police had to go on was the report that a "mysterious woman" had been heard talking with Levy outside his room on the evening of October 3, the night they believed Levy was killed. No one saw the woman—the witness only "judged by the sound of the voice" that Levy's visitor was female—but it was imperative that the police find her. They quickly did. The woman was one of Levy's tenants and had stopped by his office to pay her rent. She was cleared of any suspicion after another witness claimed to see Levy alive and well later that evening. Police had only one other lead. They followed it to Baker City, Oregon, to question a man, where it also proved fruitless.[162]

A prime suspect in Levy's murder would be in found Baker City, though. More than a week later—just over two weeks after Levy's body had been discovered—Boise law enforcement found Joe Levy (no relation to the victim), a French immigrant who lived in Boise, in the company of two prostitutes. All three were arrested.[163]

---

* The rent Levy's renters paid for a single room comes to more than $1,500 per month in today's value—a high price that rivals Boise's present-day expensive and high-demand housing market.

Several people in Boise had told the police about threats they'd heard Joe Levy, who was also known around Boise as George Levy or simply "the Frenchman," make against the deceased. Joe had been forced to leave town by police order for running a brothel. He blamed Davis for reporting him to law enforcement and "threaten[ed] dire vengeance." After hearing about the threats, police visited Joe Levy's Boise premises. There they found the same type of rope the victim had been bound and strangled with and a key that matched Davis Levy's office. Further, police discovered that Davis's second-floor rooms were accessible from a brick wall next to Joe's Boise dwelling. Muddy footprints found in Davis's building matched a set found on Joe's roof. Upon questioning, police claimed, Joe Levy told incongruous stories about his activities in the days before and after the murder. Police were "satisfied" that they'd found their man. They also amended their original thoughts on motive. Davis Levy had been murdered not for his money, but out of revenge. The dead man had been seen early the day of his murder going through the papers in the trunk, and police believed that Joe Levy staged the other evidence—the keys and the money bag—to make it appear as though robbery was the motive. The officers who arrested Joe Levy in Baker City pocketed the reward for Davis Levy's murder.[164]

This evidence, though, was circumstantial at best. The rope used to strangle the victim was a type used to secure bunches of lath, thin strips of wood used in plaster walls and roofs. Joe Levy was certainly not the only person in Boise to have some in the alley outside his dwelling. The key found outside the defendant's rooms was discovered two weeks after the crime—more than enough time for someone else to place it there. Most troubling for the prosecution, though, was Joe Levy's alibi. On the night of the murder, he had visited a barber and a cigar shop and then taken the late train to Baker City. Additionally, Joe Levy was only one man. From the beginning, police had suspected more than one person was responsible for the crime. One man could have committed the feat, the *Statesman* reported, "but it is not at all likely." The distance the body had been moved indicated "that there were at least two men, or persons, implicated in the crime."[165]

Throughout the trial, Joe Levy remained cool and calm, steadfastly holding to his innocence. After a lengthy preliminary hearing, the judge referred the case to the district court. "As a whole," he stated, "the testimony shows probable cause to believe that the defendant is guilty." This was Joe Levy's breaking point. He spent the night pacing his jail cell "like a caged lion." He "hurl[ed] anathemas at the heads of his prosecutors, protesting his innocence and begging his keepers for a revolver with which to blow out his brains." He also cried for an interpreter. One was eventually brought in—the first time the native French-speaker had been provided that service.[166]

Joe Levy's good friend, a Romanian immigrant named Bernat Edelburg, was greatly troubled by the news of Joe's plight. He was taken into custody by the police for "erratic and peculiar actions." Edelburg, according to a neighbor, kept a "light burning all night and jabbered incessantly in his native language." When visited by police, Edelburg angrily confronted the officers. "You're a bad man, you're no good, you swore against Levy, the Frenchman," he reportedly shouted in broken English. Edelburg was taken to the county jail. At a hearing to judge his sanity, Edelburg spoke calmly, answering questions about himself and Joe Levy. He steadfastly maintained the other man's innocence. After returning to his cell, however, Edelburg reportedly began "raving and jabbering in his native language." He was committed to the asylum at Blackfoot.[167]

Joe Levy's trial drew to a close in February 1902. In his closing arguments, the prosecuting attorney refuted accusations that the officers had planted evidence and arrested Joe Levy in order to reap the $4,000 reward. Additionally, he claimed the defense's star alibi witness—the cigar shop owner—was untrustworthy. He was a friend of the accused, the attorney stated, before asking the jury a leading, lingering question: "Could he have been biased in his testimony? I wonder if he could?" The jury must have

George "Joe" Levy, the man convicted of murdering Davis Levy. *P1977-2-32, "Biography—Penitentiary Inmate George Joe Levy," Idaho State Archives.*

believed so. Despite the lack of solid evidence against him, "the Frenchman" was convicted of Davis Levy's murder and sentenced to hang. His sentence was later commuted to life in prison.[168]

The case was far from settled in the eyes of many Boise citizens. In 1911, the state pardoned Joe Levy at the request of the French government and several prominent Boise businessmen. Joe Levy left Boise and was never heard of again.[169] Perhaps those in favor of the pardon had many of the same questions as today's readers: Did the police frame Joe Levy for the reward money? Were Joe Levy and Bernat Edelburg, with their broken English and troubled communication, easy scapegoats and victims of xenophobia? Was the prosecution under so much pressure to convict *someone* of the murder of one of Boise's most infamous property holders that they were willing to stretch the merely circumstantial evidence? Truth and justice remain elusive in this case, as in so many of the other transgressions that occurred in the heart of Boise's notorious red-light district—Levy's Alley.

Part III

STILLS, SMUGGLERS, CHRISTIANS AND CORRUPTION

Boise's Struggles with Prohibition

A MOVEMENT TO "TRANSFORM THE MORAL HABITS" OF THE GEM STATE

On May 8, 1894, the Boise Prohibition Club held a Demorest Medal Contest. A crowd gathered at the Baptist church to listen to the community's youth recite speeches of the most prominent leaders of the temperance movement. The night's best speaker was awarded a silver medal—"Prohibition Prize," the engraved badge proudly proclaimed. The Demorest Medal was created by William Jennings Demorest in 1886. Demorest and the organizers of contests in his name hoped that the competing youths would take the words they recited to heart and abstain from alcohol use and encourage their friends to do the same.[170]

Prostitution wasn't the only threat to upright, moral, and peaceful family life in Boise. Even before the red-light district closed in about 1910 and prostitution was no longer regulated in Boise, reformers had turned their attention to the temperance movement.[171] The Boise Prohibition Club and other reform groups claimed that alcohol came with extraordinary social costs. Alcohol use and abuse were responsible for divorce, cases of spousal and child abuse and neglect, poverty, and immoral behavior. The prohibition of alcohol could solve all of these problems, thereby making and keeping strong family life the center of American society.*

---

* Temperance is the personal decision not to drink alcohol, while prohibition refers to the legal ban of alcohol by the government. Reformers often pushed more liberal temperance platforms to win converts to their cause in the hopes of eventually enacting prohibition.

The religious fervor of the Second Great Awakening sparked the Prohibition movement. Churches like Boise's First Baptist Church, on the corner of Tenth and Jefferson, hosted speech contests, shows, speakers, and other events in support of Prohibition. *P1969-4-26, "Boise Churches—First Baptist Church," Idaho State Archives.*

Along with the Prohibition Club, Boise was also home to a chapter of the Woman's Christian Temperance Union (WCTU) and the Idaho Anti-Saloon League. The WCTU was a nationwide organization that worked to preserve the sanctity of the home. Idaho had two WCTU chapters: one in Lewiston and one in Boise. The list of social reforms pushed by the WCTU was substantial. Prostitution, labor laws, and women's rights and suffrage were among its most well known. By the turn of the twentieth century, though, the WCTU had become one of the leading organizations devoted to the temperance movement. The Anti-Saloon League was also a nationwide organization. Nonpartisan in nature, their sole issue of concern was prohibition. Boise's Prohibition Club, WCTU, and Anti-Saloon League were joined by other loosely organized reform-minded citizens, the majority of them Evangelical Christians, on a mission to rid the capital city of alcohol for good.[172]

The roots of the Prohibition movement lay in the early nineteenth century, when a wave of protestant religious revivalism swept across the United States. By 1805, the Louisiana Purchase had doubled the size of the country. The national population was growing exponentially, and millions of people were on the move to begin settling lands in the West. Protestant leaders were desperate to give migrants the tools needed to spread Christianity throughout these new territories.

Religious leaders led huge, emotional services called revivals, encouraging repentance and conversion. Converts flocked to Protestant congregations—mainly Baptist, Methodist, and Presbyterian—by the thousands. This flurry of religious ardor, known as the Second Great Awakening, led to a number of reform movements. Through social and political reform, churches hoped to "transform the moral habits of the nation." With the Second Great Awakening, religious influence in American politics increased. Some of the most pressing political issues of the nineteenth and early twentieth centuries—including abolition, women's rights, labor reform, education, and temperance—grew out of religious revival.[173]

By the twentieth century, many of the reforms begun in the ecclesiastical throes of the Second Great Awakening had borne real fruit. Slavery had been abolished, and the early labor movements of the Industrial Revolution were making headway in providing workers with more rights and benefits, including eight-hour workdays and set wages. Reform groups turned more of their attention toward temperance. In Boise, the Prohibition Club, the WCTU, and the Anti-Saloon League, with the support of most religious congregations in the Treasure Valley and statewide, were a political force to be reckoned with.

In the early twentieth century, "Sunday laws" were all the rage throughout the United States. Also called "blue laws," these were put in place to promote rest and religious activities on Sundays.* They prohibited everything from shopping and working to holding and attending nonreligious leisure activities and the sale of most items. The temperance crowd latched on to Sunday laws as a way to begin the process of total prohibition. By 1907, every state in the nation except Idaho and California had a Sunday law. Nearly all of these included restrictions on alcohol usage—namely, the sale of alcohol on Sundays. Reformers in Boise, led by the Idaho Anti-Saloon League, got to work combating the "evils of Sabbath breaking": "impurity, intemperance, and gambling."[174]

A Sunday law, its proponents argued, was not "religious legislation" that went against the "principles of American liberty." They then went on to argue, though, that "where there is no civil Sunday there tends to be no religious Sabbath and where there is no religious Sabbath there is immorality, ignorance, and tyranny." All activities, including sporting events and other "public amusements," should be prohibited so as not to "have a demoralizing effect on society." To bolster this argument, legal professionals contended that both "the federal constitution and the state constitution all recognize an overruling Providence," and Senator William Borah added that "the greatest statesman of all time taught 1900 years ago that you owe one allegiance to the law and one to the church." Despite their early statements, the Sunday law supporters' arguments all seemed based on religion. Many of the meetings—including the one in which all the preceding arguments were made—were held in churches. This hypocrisy did not prove detrimental to the cause, though. A resolution for a Sunday law was passed unanimously and was passed into law later in the legislative session.[175]

Almost immediately upon its passing, speculation began regarding the Sunday law's enforcement and constitutionality. Several of the bill's prohibitions and allowances lay in a gray area. The Ada County attorney published a letter in the *Idaho Statesman* to help explain "so many inquiries" that had come through his office regarding the new law. According to the law, the only work to be done on Sundays, he wrote, were those of "charity or necessity." "A gas company may supply gas, a water company water, a milkman deliver milk, an ice man ice," as these were businesses of necessity.

---

* Popular belief holds that the Puritans printed their Sabbath laws on blue paper or bound them in books with blue covers, hence the term "blue laws." However, no blue papers or blue-bound law books have ever been discovered. Rather, the term is probably derived from an eighteenth-century use of "blue" to describe something or someone as inflexibly moral and righteous to a negative extent.

However, "shaving, bathing, shoe shining, running street cars, have been held not to be works of necessity or charity," and so were closed. Of course, alcohol was included in the Sunday law:

> *It shall be unlawful for any person or persons in this State to keep open on Sunday any saloon, or place of any kind or description in which spirituous, vinous, malt or any intoxicating liquors are at any time sold or exposed for sale, to be sold or exposed for sale; or to give, or sell, or otherwise dispose of any spirituous, vinous, malt or any intoxicating liquors.*

Notably, the law expressly prohibited the sale and distribution of alcohol, not its consumption.[176]

If the *Statesman*'s writers are to be believed, the law was a popular success with both state government officials and the general public. "Those who demanded of the legislature the passage of such a law…number the great majority of our people," a member of the legislature wrote. "Fairly enforced," he continued, "it will meet the approval of all those who desire a decent Sunday."[177]

Popular and fairly enforced or not, the law immediately presented issues and challenges. Farmers on the Palouse in North-Central Idaho complained that it interfered with their ability to bring in the harvest. Barkeeps in the Panhandle's Silver Valley refused to close their saloons as Saturday night turned into Sunday morning. The law, one barman claimed, was "unconstitutional in that it deprived him of his property without due process of law." Enforcement was spotty. Three barkeeps in Idaho County were sentenced to a minute each in the county jail for breaking the law. In Boise, individuals were arrested for selling produce, shining shoes, and operating a bathhouse on a Sunday. When the Boise Commercial Club and Elks' Club ran their bars on Sunday, though, the Ada County attorney didn't press charges, as they were "private enterprises." Deep pockets and political influence, it seems, played into the patchwork enforcement of the Sunday law in Boise and across the state. These challenges and inconsistencies didn't perturb the law's proponents, though. Instead, they pushed forward in support of more legislation to regulate the use of alcohol within Idaho.[178]

Reformers sought a gradual tightening of rules surrounding alcohol use on their path toward total prohibition. In May 1908, just a year after the passage of the Sunday law, representatives of the Anti-Saloon League, Prohibition Party, Woman's Christian Temperance Union, and others met in Boise to discuss the "next great thing for which they would work": a local option for counties and precincts.[179]

A local option law would give each municipal jurisdiction within the state—city or county—the ability for their voters to decide the limits of alcohol prohibition within that area. Through a local option, the voters could choose what types of alcohol could be sold, where and when. Sales could be limited to groceries or saloons; consumption could be relegated to on- or off-premises; and beer, wine, and spirits could all be limited or prohibited, together or individually. The local option allowed individual jurisdictions to control alcohol use in any way that they wished.[180]

The local option was brought up for official discussion and a vote during the Idaho legislative session of 1909. The debate was heated, and accusations of treachery and double-dealing flew across the aisle. Some legislators speculated about various possible amendments. Some of these, detractors warned, would make the entire bill useless. No one seemed to know which party planned to introduce said amendments—Democrats and Republicans

The Woman's Christian Temperance Movement played a huge role in regulating prostitution and the passage of Prohibition in Idaho. Pictured is President Nettie Chip in the state headquarters office of the Idaho WTCU, circa 1916. *P1960-114-7, "Boise Associations—Woman's Christian Temperance Union, Idaho President Mrs. Chipp," Idaho State Archives.*

alike both accused and denied. Finally, the senate finished discussing the bill and recommended its passage, with several amendments, just five minutes before the end of a long, tense day. The senate minority "was given little consideration in amending the bill," and "urgent appeals...to amend the bill...were firmly but speedily snubbed." The governor promised to give the pen used to sign the legislation to the leaders of Idaho's Woman's Christian Temperance Union.[181]

Saloonkeepers in Boise and around the state were obviously unhappy with the outcome. In the months and weeks leading up the September 8 local option vote, they waged an information campaign that, if reports are to be believed, turned personal and slanderous in nature. Governor Brady, Boise barkeeps claimed, was a hypocrite. Idaho's chief executive regularly imbibed and served alcohol to guests in his home, they postulated. Furthermore, "the den in the cellar at the executive mansion is a storehouse for liquors of all kinds," kept for sale and the governor's personal use. Governor Brady vehemently disagreed. "I have never served wine in my home," he declared, "and never expect to." The rumors of a secret liquor warehouse in the governor's mansion were "absolutely false," and "the saloonmen know it." Boise's bar owners, the governor alleged, were simply trying to throw the local option bill into a negative light. "As long as I am chief executive of this state," Governor Brady continued, "I shall advocate prohibition and the cause of temperance."[182]

Some saloons tried other tactics. All of the bars in Idaho Falls, save one, voluntarily closed for the days leading up to the election. They hoped to "give people a touch of closed town" to sway votes against the local option.[183] Other businessmen joined the saloonkeepers in their opposition. One Boise businessman claimed that even the consideration of Ada County "going dry" had a negative effect on business. He was familiar with different cities in Colorado, which experienced a lull in all businesses following votes to go dry. If Ada County voted for the local option, he claimed, "the people and business men will regret it." The man failed, though, to cite any specific examples or evidence of business woes that local prohibition had caused.[184]

September 8, Election Day for Ada and some other counties in Idaho, arrived, and both sides were "confident that victory will be theirs."[185] Large voter turnout was expected for this momentous decision. People made bets, and the question of wet versus dry divided families and communities. The division was apparent when the votes were counted. Ada County stayed wet. Neighboring Canyon County went dry. By the end of the year, more jurisdictions had voted. Thirteen of Idaho's twenty-three counties elected to go dry; only two—Ada and Elmore—remained wet. Saloons around the state were given until the next spring before they would be forced to close.[186]

In Boise, the battle was far from over. Less than a month after Ada County's contentious vote, the mayor removed the police chief and a police sergeant of duty. The move was completely unexpected—"like a bolt from a clear sky." The removal, the mayor said, "was for the good of the service." He refused to address speculation that he believed the chief had mishandled "the saloon situation" and that the sergeant was "too wet." Both officers refused to resign, instead letting the mayor fire them. The chief wanted to "get out of this misery" as soon as possible. Given the option of resigning, the sergeant simply turned and walked out of the mayor's office. The two former officers had no doubts as to the reason for their firing. "It is the old political game," the ex-chief said, "and it looks to me a frame-up." "The whole thing is funny to me," the ex-sergeant simply stated. If the mayor were playing a political game related to the local option, he would have a few more high-profile "wet" city appointees to dismiss, including the fire chief, a police captain, a street commissioner, and a city engineer.[187]

One of the city's reverends encouraged his congregation to "lay aside all feelings of bitterness and hatred," language that demonstrates just how divided the city's populace was on the issue. "Let us quietly abide by the decision of the majority," he pleaded. The "wets" had just the same rights to an opinion as the "drys," he added. The good reverend continued his sermon with a hopeful note. "I am convinced," he told his flock, "that whereas with Ada county prohibition we would have banished saloons from Boise, in statewide prohibition we will be able to banish saloons and breweries from the whole of Idaho." The reverend believed that this defeat was only temporary and might simply be paving the way for total prohibition.[188]

Less than a decade later, the people and the governor's pen spoke on the matter again.

RUMRUNNERS, HIDDEN HOOTCH AND AN INTOXICATED COYOTE

A well-dressed little girl took her place in front of a packed house at Boise's Pinney Theatre in October 1916. After witnessing a performance by a girls' chorus and recitations by other children, the audience surely wondered what this small girl's talent was. The girl had no lines to recite, though. She simply held a placard reading, "My papa will vote dry for me." She pranced proudly offstage and was immediately replaced by a similarly aged and sized boy bearing his own placard. He, however, was poorly dressed, possibly a bit unkempt—an orphan, the audience surely assumed. His placard read, "Will you vote dry for me?"[189]

Just as the reverend and many other prohibition advocates predicted, the 1909 local option vote was not the end of the fight against the moral ills of alcohol in Boise. The Woman's Christian Temperance Union, Anti-Saloon League, Prohibition Party (of which Idaho's new governor, Moses Alexander, was a member), and others kept their crusade going, and in 1916, they were ready to try again.

The arguments were very similar if not refined. Prohibition would keep home life and families whole and together, would reduce the crime rate and number of arrests and would lead to lower taxes because those social ills wouldn't need tax-funded services and reforms. The temperance crowd also, again, accused the wet supporters of underhanded dealings. "Outside liquor interests," they claimed, were attempting to "flood the state with booze" to counteract the prohibitionists. Although men were arrested and liquor confiscated in dry counties, there was little evidence that these activities were part of "concerted efforts" to "discredit prohibition in Idaho."[190]

Most Idahoans were strongly in the prohibitionists' corner. The 1909 local option votes may have been close in many counties, but the statewide prohibition vote was a completely different story. Almost three quarters (71 percent) of the voters placed their ballots in favor of total statewide prohibition. All of the individual counties voted in favor of the amendment. More than 60 percent of voters chose prohibition in every county.[191]

How had sentiment changed so much in Idaho in less than a decade? One explanation could be the population shift. Nearly 100,000 people moved into the Idaho between 1909 and 1916. The demographics, specifically regarding economics, changed. Miners left the played-out areas of the Boise Basin and the Owyhees. More farmers and ranchers moved into the state, and the towns and cities grew larger. Farmers, merchants, and livestock growers brought their families with them to settle into their city homes and rural homesteads. This trend toward domesticity had already begun in 1909. By 1916, it was much further along. The rough-and-tumble, Wild West, vigilante days of Idaho were over. Idahoans had decided that they wanted law, order, and strong morality based around family to be the basis of life in the Gem State.

The prohibition vote may have been decisive, but it didn't mean that, leading up to it, Idahoans had no desire to use alcohol. In early 1917, the US

Governor Moses Alexander signs the Prohibition Bill (H.B. 142) on March 1, 1915, surrounded by his grandchildren, members of the Anti-Saloon League, WTCU, ministry, and legislature. *P1960-114-9, "Governor Moses Alexander Signing Prohibition Bill," Idaho State Archives.*

Treasury Department reported that, according to tax returns, Americans consumed more whiskey in 1916 than they had in any year since 1909. Those numbers do not account for the amount of alcohol produced, and then subsequently consumed, by "off the books" illegal stills. Americans, and certainly Idahoans, though outwardly favoring prohibition, still inwardly embraced alcohol.[192]

The ink had barely dried on governor's signature on the prohibition bill before Boiseans began to look for ways to skirt the law. Since Idaho was the only state in the nation at the time to embrace total prohibition, much of the illegal alcohol came from out of state. Boise detectives took to searching the train cars that pulled into town. During an early morning raid in January 1917, detectives "armed with a search warrant" boarded a train as it arrived. They searched each passenger's suitcase for booze but came up with nothing. "The bird, if there had been one," the *Idaho Statesman* wrote, "had flown."[193]

The tips police received regarding booze transport by train were sometimes correct. In April 1917, police arrested three men—Orrie Cole, the owner of auto dealership; one of his drivers; and a railroad porter—for smuggling whiskey. The contraband in question had come by train from Ogden, Utah. Boise police, "having reason to believe there was liquor" on the train, watched from a distance as a car pulled up next to where the locomotive was stopped at the freight depot. When Cole and the porter began moving cases of liquor from the train to the vehicle, the police swooped in. At trial, Cole's lawyer argued that his client had merely been conducting a transaction related to his auto business. He didn't know the luggage contained liquor. The jury deliberated for only thirty minutes before finding Cole not guilty of "the possession and transportation of intoxicating liquor." Whether they bought Cole's story or were loath to sentence an influential businessman is unknown. Writers at the *Idaho Statesman* withheld judgment.[194]

After getting liquor into Idaho, smugglers faced another challenge: where to store their goods. The Nevada-to-Boise route through Bruneau seemed a popular one with southern Idaho bootleggers. In the spring of 1917, Ada County sheriff Emmett Pfost and another officer tailed two suspected rumrunners through Owyhee County. Both were stopped and arrested as soon as they crossed the Ada County line. Their "nearly new" cars were filled with booze. The police confiscated the haul, worth almost $64,000 in today's money, and the cars.[195]

In August of that same year, police had an interview with a young man. In a written statement, the man said that he'd been hired to drive a truck from Bruneau to Boise. Until he arrived for the job, he hadn't been aware of the truck's contents. When the boss handed him a bottle of beer, though, he learned what his cargo included. He drove the goods—"five barrels of whisky and eight boxes of bottled beer"—into the capital city for storage. Early on a Sunday morning, he followed Broadway to the north side of the Boise River and turned into Julia Davis Park. The contraband was stored in a swampy area close to the riverbank. Lawmen immediately went on the hunt for the illegal liquor. They found the spot, evidenced by divots in the ground where whiskey barrels had been rolled in and out of position. All that was left of the load was a whiskey barrel and three beer boxes. All were empty. The police weren't totally out of luck, though. Their witness had provided them with vital details, including names and a delivery point. Days later, authorities arrested two men outside Bruneau who'd just crossed the state line from Nevada in a truck carrying liquor worth approximately $2,600 (almost $54,000 today). This cache, more than thirty cases in total, was certainly bound for the bank of the Boise River in Julia Davis Park. The young man who led the cops to the first cache had given away the entire operation.[196]

Some bootleggers were foiled not by informants but by their own bad luck. In June 1918, a man named Richard Tucker was brought into a Boise hospital with severe bruising around his upper body. Tucker had wrecked his auto on the highway about fourteen miles east of Boise. He was dazed and "not well aware of his surroundings" and allowed Sheriff Pfost to accompany him to the accident scene. There, with Tucker's overturned vehicle, they found a dozen bottles of whiskey, two of which had broken and spilled in the accident. Tucker was immediately arrested.[197]

In another case of bad luck, police in Meridian found a suitcase full of "booze-dampened clothing of the feminine variety." The trunk had originated in Nampa and was supposed to be picked up in Meridian. Before the parcel could be claimed, though, people in the station baggage room noticed the tell-tale smell of liquor. Police were called and pulled eleven full bottles from the trunk. A twelfth had broken, soaking the trunk's other contents in booze. Sheriff Pfost confiscated the liquor but balked at the "Woman's Apparel." The trunk of liquor-soaked lingerie was left to wait for its claimant.[198]

Sometimes bootleggers simply choose the wrong hiding place for their illegal wares. A farmer in Caldwell went out one summer evening to water his garden only to discover that his irrigation system wasn't working correctly. Instead of the usual strong, steady flow, the water slowly trickled through the pipes. Upon investigation, the farmer discovered the problem. The irrigation ditch was clogged, not with mud or other natural debris, but with "a sack containing 24 bottles of whisky." The farmer removed the sack from the ditch and watered his garden. The next day, he contacted police. The Canyon County sheriff "added the booze to his elaborate and growing collection."[199]

In another instance, bootleggers who had stashed "44 quarts of perfectly good booze in some sagebrush outside of Nampa" were foiled by thirsty wildlife. Early one morning, a coyote stumbled into town. Police reported the animal "looked bleary-eyed and its breath smelled of booze." Police decided to set the coyote free, sure that it would return to "the seat of his happiness." Sure enough, the animal led authorities to a liquor cache in the shade of some sagebrush. The owner of the liquor, the police cheekily announced, could have it back by "applying in person to Chief of Police Larry Maloney, city hall, Nampa, Ida." The coyote was not charged.[200]

Idaho's bootleggers got quite creative and enterprising in their efforts to distribute booze. In 1918, Canyon County officials discovered an "underground railroad" moving confiscated liquor from a vault in the county

The old Union Pacific Depot, built in 1893, stood at Tenth and Front Streets. Bootleggers often used the railroad to move illegal booze from out of state and across the Treasure Valley. *P1969-4-40b(2), "Boise Railroads—Train at Old Passenger Depot," Idaho State Archives.*

courthouse to the outside world for redistribution. Somehow, an inmate in the Canyon County Jail discovered the combination to the vault while in the courthouse for his trial proceedings. On each visit to the courthouse, he would "take some of the goods" and then "leave them behind the jail" for an outside accomplice to pick up before he returned to his cell. This was a bold, if not foolhardy, operation for the men to undertake on their own. Certainly, they must have had help from the inside. No law enforcement officer, jailer or courthouse staffer was implicated in the scheme, though.[201]

Simply because no official was involved or implicated in the Canyon County courthouse plot doesn't mean that the authorities weren't sometimes involved with the illegal side of bootlegging. Cora Gaskell began working for the Boise Police Department in 1917. She was a "special policewoman," appointed by the mayor to "protect young girls from immoral women" for ten dollars a week. More than law enforcement, her job was more one of community outreach and social work. By July 1918, though, Gaskell, no longer with the police department, had been arrested four times "on a charge of having intoxicating liquors." Each time, she was released without a conviction. Even after searching her Eighth Street property, police couldn't find any evidence that she purchased, distributed or made her own liquor.[202]

Nearly a year later, though, police again charged Gaskell with selling liquor. Just a week after this arrest, they discovered a distillery at her home near Julia Davis Park. Officers found 174 quarts of whiskey and a home-brewing operation. Gaskell brewed her own beer by stewing hops and malt on her gas range. Then she placed the mixture in a stone jar to ferment before filtering and bottling. Police confiscated 20 quart-size bottles of beer and four gallons still unbottled. The whiskey was hidden under her house; a trapdoor led to a small storage space. Perhaps this was where all of the liquor had been hidden during the previous raids on Gaskell's home.[203]

Gaskell's charges for selling liquor were dismissed for lack of evidence, but she pleaded guilty to having intoxicating liquor in her possession. She was sentenced to thirty days in jail and a $450 fine (almost $7,000 today). If she did not or was unable to pay the fine, Gaskell was ordered to "serve it out in jail at $2 per day."[204]

Although she may have been the first caught, it's likely that Cora Gaskell wasn't the first Boise official involved in a bootlegging scheme, and she certainly wouldn't be the last.

CROOKED COPS AND METICULOUS NOTE-TAKING

By the time the United States ratified the Eighteenth Amendment declaring nationwide Prohibition, Idaho was already three years into the "great social and economic experiment."[205] Things hadn't exactly panned out as well as the members of the Anti-Saloon League, Woman's Christian Temperance Union, Prohibition Party, and others planned, though. Bootlegging was rampant in southern Idaho, and in the early 1920s, the situation grew even more rife with corruption.

By 1923, Emmett Pfost had retired his position as sheriff, and James D. Agnew had taken over the job. Agnew was a well-respected lawman. In January 1923, he attended the convention of the Northwest Sheriff's Association in Portland, where he was named chairman of the association's legislative committee and held a seat on several other committees. Just a month later, though, Boise was shocked when Sheriff Agnew was indicted on six counts of manufacturing and selling liquor. Among those indicted with him were Deputy Sheriff Sylvester Kinney; Boise Chief of Police Henry Griffith; Boise police detective Ed Hill; Dr. H. Goodfriend, a prominent Boise physician; Carl and Edith Sorenson, who managed a rooming house; and several local businessmen. The ensuing events uncovered corruption at the highest levels since Dave Updyke had his run-in with the vigilantes almost sixty years earlier.

All defendants were arrested immediately on the following counts:

Count No. 1 charges all conspired together in the possession for sale for beverage purposes of certain intoxicating liquor commonly known as "moonshine whisky."

Count No. 2 charges all conspired to engage in the business of selling at retail and wholesale certain intoxicating liquors.

Count No. 3 charges all willfully manufactured certain intoxicating liquors for beverages purposes.

Count No. 4 charges all defendants had in their possession and custody a certain still and distilling apparatus without having registered the same with the internal revenue collector for Idaho.

Count No. 5 charges all carried on the business of a distiller without having given the bond required by law with intent to defraud the United States of the tax on the "spirits distilled by them."

Count No. 6 charges all defendants did willfully and unlawfully "make and ferment in a building and on premises other than a distillery, duly authorized according to law, 500 gallons of mash, wort and mash, fit for distillation and designed and intended for the production of spirits and alcohol."[206]

Most of the parties involved vehemently denied any involved.

"I haven't the remotest idea of my connection with any liquor conspiracy," Deputy Kinney told the *Statesman*.

"I am absolutely innocent," Chief Griffith claimed. "So far as I know there is nothing to the charge."

"I can't say anything…because I don't know what it is all about," Detective Hill stated.

"There is evidence of a plot," Dr. Goodfriend declared. "I have known for months that there was a plot brewing and the evidence in the case will show a plot."

The Boise mayor and Sheriff Agnew echoed Goodfriend's sentiments. Police officers, the mayor stated, "are always the object of temptation," and they were also "often the target of slander and blackmail," especially the most "officient [*sic*]" officers. He suspected that the evidence would reveal a situation "tinged with political blackmail."

Sheriff Agnew had been at dinner at the Owyhee Hotel with his wife when he was arrested. "I know of no reason why I should have been publicly and unnecessarily humiliated and degraded," Sheriff Agnew said. In fact, Agnew claimed, most of the more than one hundred arrests he'd made in his two years as sheriff had been part of prohibition enforcement. These activities had made him "a host of bitter political and personal enemies," and a full investigation would bring them to light.[207]

All of the defendants pleaded not guilty to the charges.[208] As the defendants' lawyers prepared for trial, they asked the judge for more information. What exactly, they wondered, was the nature of the evidence against their clients? Had all of them been accused of personally selling liquor? Did all of the defendants hatch this alleged conspiracy together, or did some join in after it was up and running? How was the supposed ring run and from where? Without that information, the defense felt they were going into trial blind. The federal judge overseeing the case, though, declined to provide any details.[209]

The trial opened to a courtroom packed with spectators. The prosecutors began by escorting "a massive pile of moonshining apparatus," barrels and bottles of illegal whiskey confiscated throughout the investigation, and a parade of federal prohibition agents into the courtroom. The jury was confronted head-on with the evidence of the defendants' wrongdoings. Prosecutors then outlined their case:

> *That Dr. Henry Goodfriend, Boise physician and one of the alleged ring and that all of the defendants met frequently in his office to discuss the business and developments and plans for carrying on an unlawful liquor business.*
>
> *That Sheriff Agnew was a party to the manufacture of liquor seized… next door to the suburban home of Doctor Goodfriend….That the sheriff*

furnished the defendant, Ed Kemp, with barrels for the work and that Kemp "saw" the sheriff relative to the business.

That federal agents saw and heard Chief Griffith and the doctor in converse relative to "protection" for…hotels charged to the principal dispensaries of liquor for the alleged ring.

That Agnew, Kemp and Deputy Sheriff Sylvester Kinney were to do the active work of the manufacturing of liquor.

That Agnew and the physician were heard to discuss profits of the business and were heard to say that they planned to…start on a larger scale.

That all the members of the alleged ring were impressed with their duty of running all other bootleggers and moonshiners out of town for the collective benefit of those engaged in the "ring." That in doing this, the sheriff and chief of police were to have one of their men on every raid carried on by the federal agents.

That money was seen to pass hands in Doctor Goodfriend's office among members of the ring.

…That he [Agnew] told Goodfriend in the case of the Union rooming house arrests, for sale of liquors, that he [Agnew] would get "favorable jurors."

That the Union and Vernon rooms were to act as the dispensing points for the "ring's" moonshine, that they planned to start a "gallon route" in Boise and extend their activities to other towns.[210]

The charges and the details prosecutors claimed to have about the ring were astounding. After their opening "theatrical presentation," the prosecution's star witness took the stand. Mrs. Marie Curtis worked with her husband in an office next to Dr. Goodfriend's private practice in the Empire Building. She had overheard several suspicious conversations coming from the doctor's office, Mrs. Curtis said, and reported them to federal prohibition officials. The Curtises had even helped the federal investigation, she reported, with the installation of a "detectograph"—an early audio recording device—under Dr. Goodfriend's desk when he was out one day. With this news, the courtroom erupted in a frenzied burst of objections by defense attorneys. The judge agreed with the defense's assertions the detectograph's placement had been unconstitutional. Mrs. Curtis was allowed to continue her testimony, limited to only what she'd heard "through cracks in the door" and not with the device.[211]

Mrs. Curtis—"pretty" and "charmingly tailored"—had everyone's rapt attention. "Jurors leaned forward motionless, spectators were silent," and

Dr. Goodfriend's office in the Empire Building, on the corner of Tenth and Idaho (pictured here in the early twentieth century), was right next to the office where Mrs. Curtis worked in, giving her a prime location from which to gather information. *P1962-20-01, "Boise Buildings—Empire," Idaho State Archives.*

"all three members of the prosecutor's staff leaned back smiling" as she explained how she had worked with federal investigators to gather more evidence about the doctor's bootlegging operation. Even without the recorded conversations, she had plenty to say. She had even taken copious notes, Mrs. Curtis indicated. She pulled out a notebook and began to read aloud as if from a novel.[212]

The previous fall, Mrs. Curtis relayed, she'd overheard two men discussing a still. They talked about where to set one up and what materials were needed. She was curious, Mrs. Curtis said, so she "climbed on a chair and peered through a crack." She identified Dr. Goodfriend and another defendant, Ed Kemp, as the men who'd been talking about the illegal operation. Over the next months, through the cracks in the doorway, Mrs. Curtis also witnessed conversations between Goodfriend, Sheriff Agnew, Deputy Kinney, Chief Griffith, and both of the Sorensons, owners of the hotels identified by prosecutors. The woman read entire conversations from her notebook, written word-for-word in narrative style. At different points in time, the doctor discussed various ways of distributing illegal liquor with Sheriff Agnew and still operations with Mr. Sorenson. Goodfriend and Chief Griffith talked about a member of police force who was causing some trouble for their operation; Griffith summarily kicked the officer in question off the force. Mrs. Sorenson came to Goodfriend because "she was so nervous she didn't know what to do" about liquor-related arrests in her hotels. The doctor managed to assuage her fears, and Sheriff Agnew vowed that he "would get 'favorable jurors'" for those trials. Deputy Kinney and Goodfriend discussed different members of the ring and their associates, debated who they could and could not trust and plotted to have the bond lowered for an associated arrested on a liquor charge. Curious Mrs. Curtis and her notebook had confirmed all of the prosecutors' claims. The jury hung on her every word. The prosecution rested after her testimony.[213]

The drama continued with the defendants' turn to present their case. A rumor began to circulate through Boise that Sheriff Agnew "had turned 'state's evidence,'" and almost three hundred people crowded into the courtroom to find out what would happen. They crammed into the seats and stood in every bit of open floor space. Some sat on window ledges until the bailiffs warned them off. Those who couldn't fit in the courtroom gathered in a "dense mob" in the hallway outside.[214]

The rumors about the sheriff turned out to be unsubstantiated, but the massive crowd still got a good show. Sheriff Agnew, Chief Griffith, Deputy Kinney, and Mr. Sorenson all took their turns on the witness stand, each flatly denying all the charges against them. Yes, they'd visited Dr. Goodfriend's office, each admitted, but not for the purposes of discussing an illegal booze operation. Mrs. Curtis, they all indicated, without actually mentioning her or any of her testimony, had simply misunderstood what she'd heard. Any discussions with Dr. Goodfriend were about other crimes and situations the doctor knew of because of his prominent standing in town. Each defendant spoke calmly and with conviction. Chief Griffith's testimony was, the *Statesman* reported, "impregnable." The prosecution was unable to "catch" or shake the defendants on cross-examination. All of them except Deputy Kinney.[215]

Deputy Kinney had, he confirmed, been often to Dr. Goodfriend's office. The deputy spoke with the doctor about "immorality and the liquor traffic and so forth" in both personal and professional capacities. Dr. Goodfriend, Kinney stated, had information about liquor trafficking that the deputy needed in order to fulfil his professional duties. On a personal level, though, the deputy appreciated Dr. Goodfriend's donations and other work toward the prohibition cause. Kinney was "strongly moved by emotion" as he testified about his desire to have his son grow up free of the immoralities liquor caused. The doctor's good deeds and support helped reassure him through times of "nervous trouble."[216]

The *Statesman*'s reporters failed to mention the prosecution's reaction to the cracks in Kinney's façade. They also did not state whether the jury was moved or not by Kinney's emotional display, but they did take note of the jurors' reactions when the charismatic "brains" of the bootlegging operation took the stand. Dr. Goodfriend spoke in a "strong voice, his face masked." Occasionally, he showed "amused wonderment at some of the prosecution's allegations." The doctor held the audience in suspense and at times "provoked gales of laughter" that the visibly amused bailiffs struggled to contain. He made a good witness.[217]

Dr. Goodfriend denied all of the prosecution's assertions, claiming innocence not only for himself but also for his co-defendants. Mrs. Sorenson, he claimed, was a patient of his, afflicted with a terrible nervous condition. The poor woman had made suicidal threats in the past and was, at the moment, confined to her bed. He'd spoken with most of the other defendants as well at various times. He and Deputy Kinney had indeed discussed local liquor traffic, "social diseases" and the moral ills "among Boise's youth."[218]

Dr. Goodfriend did admit to a one-time involvement in trafficking liquor. He had taken it upon himself to try to trace three bottles of whiskey through one of Sheriff Agnew's deputies. He'd even spoken with the prosecuting attorney about this, he testified nonchalantly. "I called them state's exhibits 1, 2, and 3," he added, yawning. Nothing ever came of his vigilante operation. This particular deputy was the reason he had campaigned against Sheriff Agnew's election, Dr. Goodfriend said. He "didn't want to be arrested by a professional bootlegger." After Agnew had been elected, though, the two began working together to root out illegal booze. In short, the good doctor had an answer for every accusation thrown his way.[219]

At closing arguments, prosecutors attacked Dr. Goodfriend first. The doctor had testified with patronizing amusement, and the prosecutor argued against him with sarcasm. Goodfriend was the one "who contributes to the 'Y' and the churches, the Sunday school and the church organizations! He… goes on all the bootleggers' bonds!" the prosecutor announced, "smiling cynically." He then questioned why Sheriff Agnew would be friendly with someone who'd campaigned against him if there was no monetary benefit. As for Deputy Kinney, he was a "weakling," the prosecutor pronounced. Kinney was "susceptible to an approach and bribery" because of "his illness and debts" and lack of "strength and integrity."[220]

The bootleggers' ring was a plot "at the very foundations of your government," the prosecutor told the jury. The operation was foiled, though, thanks to the honesty and integrity of Mrs. Curtis. The defendants' attorneys had been unable to poke holes in her story because there were none. The defense, the prosecutor alleged, had tried to attack her personally but only ended in making her a more sympathetic, believable figure. The defendants' primary goal had been to control all liquor traffic in Boise, but Mrs. Curtis had put a stop to the conspiracy. Her actions had helped "rid the community of such corruption."[221]

The defense used the majority of its closing arguments to attack Mrs. Curtis. She was not a good and moral citizen doing her duty, but rather a meddlesome eavesdropper. Mrs. Curtis, the defense claimed, reveled in the attention the investigation had brought her. She "enjoyed her position, standing in the limelight." Before all of this, she was a completely unknown character. Further, the defense alleged, Mrs. Curtis's actions—eavesdropping and "'peeping' into a doctor's office"—were reprehensible. Would the jury convict these fine men—a well-known and good doctor, a respected lawmen and honest businessmen—on the word of one woman and abusive questioning from an over-ambitious prosecutor?[222]

The closing arguments were personal and ugly. Dr. Goodfriend's testimony was affable and entertaining, and the other defendants never strayed from their denials. Mrs. Curtis was charming and thorough. Who would the jury believe? The enormous crowd waited in the courtroom for more than six hours—until after 1:00 a.m.—to hear the answer. The courtroom was nearly silent when the jury delivered guilty verdicts for Dr. Goodfriend, Sheriff Agnew, Deputy Kinney, Mr. Sorenson, and two others. Agnew "greeted his conviction with a set jaw," and Kinney "nervously stroked his chin with one hand." Chief Griffith and Detective Hill, the latter of which was never mentioned in the trial, were acquitted.

Mrs. Sorenson "was not considered in this case" at all, as she was "ill in bed." A final defendant was never brought to trial.

As the leader of the operation, Goodfriend was sentenced to fifteen months in the federal penitentiary at McNeil's Island, Washington, and fined $2,000. Agnew was given a fine of $1,000 and ten months in the Canyon County Jail. Kinney, Sorenson, and the other guilty defendants were ordered six months in the Canyon County Jail and fines of $500.[223]

Boise's biggest and most infamous prohibition case drew to an end, but it wasn't the end of illegal booze operations in the Treasure Valley. Alcohol remained in demand, so bootlegging continued. Prohibition hurt the American economy, as black market alcohol became its own economic force. Thousands of brewers, distillers, and others involved even peripherally in the alcohol trade were left unemployed. Some restaurants and theaters were unable to turn a profit. The prohibition law against manufacturing, selling, and transporting alcohol left one big loophole open, though: it was still legal to consume and purchase liquor. As long as people could find alcohol, it was perfectly legal to drink it.[224]

Other loopholes soon became apparent. Pharmacists could give out whiskey to treat "any number of ailments, ranging from anxiety to influenza." Pharmacies were a perfect cover for illicit liquor trade. Alcohol, in the form of sacramental wine, was not only an allowed but also an expected part of many religious ceremonies. Some historians have found that church enrollments rose, as did the number of religious leaders who were able to obtain wine for services.[225]

Home stills were technically illegal, but Americans could find the materials needed to build one in hardware stores, and distilling instructions were readily available in pamphlets from the U.S. Department of Agriculture. Instead of stopping Americans from drinking alcohol, Prohibition was "turning many of them into experts on how to make it." The alcohol made in home stills posed a new public health problem. The quality of much of this unregulated liquor had dire health effects. Jamaican ginger, commonly known as "jake," was used in many patent medicines. When used improperly, as it often was in illegal distilling operations run by novice distillers, the 70–80 percent alcohol extract could cause a neurological issue commonly called "jake leg." Victims experienced partial paralysis that began in the feet and ended in the inability to walk or even death. Other additives to illegal booze, including castor oil and other chemical additives, caused a plethora of other health problems. Historians estimate that tainted liquor killed an average of one thousand people each year of Prohibition.[226]

Prohibition shut down all of Boise's saloons, like this one (circa 1910), and not only put bartenders and brewers out of work but also led to the mass unemployment of others—like bottlers, waiters, and barrel makers—who also made a living from the alcohol trade. *P1974-153-5d, "Liquor Traffic in Boise, 1910," Idaho State Archives.*

After thirteen years of corruption, economic issues, health problems and uneven enforcement, America put an end to the failed Prohibition experiment. Boise's saloonkeepers opened their doors, home brewers and distillers exchanged their subpar liquor for the better booze they could now get in shops again, and law enforcement officers turned their attentions to other issues. Prohibition may have ended, but that experiment was not the only time Idaho passed a law aimed at "correcting" the moral habits of its residents.

Part IV

MORALITY AND MOTIVE

Morals Laws and the Unclear Question of Intent

THE PUNISHMENT FITS THE CRIME?

Fred Dubois was on a mission. Born into privilege in Illinois in 1851, Dubois coupled his family's connections (his father was a friend of Abraham Lincoln) with his natural ambition to make a name for himself. He held minor political appointments in Illinois and then followed his brother west. Broke for the first time in his life, Dubois took a job as a cowboy, driving cattle between Blackfoot, Idaho, and Casper, Wyoming. The rigors of the trail were Dubois's first taste of frontier life. He returned to Blackfoot and worked odd jobs, gaining even more knowledge and appreciation for Idaho Territory's rough ways, and, most importantly, making friends and allies. In 1881, Dubois decided that he wanted to bring law and order to the territory. Like most of his previous occupations, Dubois jumped into law enforcement with little knowledge and a great deal of help from powerful and influential friends. Robert Todd Lincoln helped Dubois get appointed U.S. marshal of Idaho Territory.[227]

Now one of the most powerful men in the territory, Dubois set to work immediately. Despite its smaller population, Idaho, he said, had "more criminals than the State of Illinois."[228] He chased down cattle thieves, stage robbers, murderers, and swindlers. Dubois's biggest criminal target, though, was the Mormons.

Since the founding of the Church Jesus Christ of Latter-day Saints (LDS) in 1830, its members were in near constant conflict with their communities.

The Mormons established large communities, and their non-Mormon neighbors opposed the economic and political competition. Most anti-Mormon sentiment, though, stemmed from the beliefs preached by LDS leaders. All other Christian denominations, LDS missionaries claimed, were illegitimate. Theirs was the only "true church."[229] These statements obviously enflamed the ire of others. The biggest mark against the Mormons, in non-Mormon eyes, was the practice of polygamy.

Fred DuBois used his family's political connections to land the job of U.S. marshal of Idaho Territory. DuBois used his position to promote and enforce laws, like those against bigamy and polygamy, to disenfranchise Mormons. He later served represented Idaho for two terms in the U.S. Senate. *P1148-5, "Biography—Fred T. Dubois," Idaho State Archives.*

The Mormons moved from Upstate New York west to Ohio, Missouri, Illinois, and finally Utah, running from anti-Mormon prejudice and violence and gaining followers along the way. The Saints finally found peace in the late 1840s, settling the wide Salt Lake Valley and founding many communities up and down the Wasatch Range through Utah and southeastern Idaho. This quiet calm was not to last, though. Word traveled east that the LDS Church was still not only teaching but also openly practicing polygamy. In 1856, the Republican Party was created on the platform of abolishing the "twin relics of barbarism": slavery and polygamy. The fight against slavery was terrible and bloody, leaving physical and emotional scars across the nation, some of which, arguably, have not yet healed. The war against polygamy, though, was fought mainly in courtrooms and the halls of Congress.[230]

In 1862, Congress passed the Morrill Act for the Suppression of Polygamy, also known as the Morrill Anti-Bigamy Act, as a reaction to the rumors coming out of Utah.* The law, though, was difficult to enforce. Two decades later, a year after Dubois's appointment, Congress passed the Edmunds Act of 1882, outlawing "unlawful cohabitation." With this measure, polygamists could no longer skirt the law by entering only one legal marriage but having multiple church-endorsed marriages. The Edmunds Act effectively prohibited plural marriages in all forms.

---

* Polygamy is having more than one spouse at the same time, while bigamy is going through a marriage ceremony while still married to another person. One must commit bigamy in order to commit polygamy.

In Idaho, Dubois enforced the Edmunds Act with zeal. "Every member of the Mormon Church was a criminal either actually in practice or as an accessory," he declared. Dubois had a problem, though, as in many southeastern Idaho communities, the Mormons largely outnumbered the non-Mormons. Finding a jury that would convict on a polygamy charge, then, became almost impossible. Dubois's solution was to champion *open venire*. This gave him, as the marshal, the ability to choose who would sit on juries. Dubois's anti-Mormon juries went on to successfully convict dozens of Mormons of polygamy.[231]

The LDS Church formally renounced the practice of polygamy in 1890, paving the way for Utah's statehood in 1896. In 1904, the church strictly forbade plural marriages among its members. Now, Mormons caught practicing polygamy are excommunicated.[232]

Although the roots of the bigamy and polygamy laws lie in anti-Mormonism, the Mormons who followed the practice of plural marriage weren't the only Idahoans who ran afoul of them. In November 1915, Edward Cooper married an "estimable young woman" named Hannah Kellerman. Kellerman had managed to save several hundred dollars through her work as a housekeeper, but her new husband absconded with the money less than a week after the wedding. He was arrested in Portland in March 1916 and brought back to Boise to serve a sixty-day sentence in the Ada County Jail for "wife desertion." Upon his release in June, though, Cooper found his legal troubles only beginning. He was again arrested almost immediately and charged with bigamy. Cooper, the prosecuting attorney claimed, had already been married when he'd said his vows to Hannah Kellerman. The prosecutor was right. Cooper had a wife and three children in Utah and pleaded guilty to the charge. He was sentenced to the Idaho State Penitentiary for a period of six months to five years. The judge annulled his marriage to Kellerman at the young woman's request. Cooper was paroled after serving six months of his sentence. Whether he returned to his wife and children in Utah is unknown.[233]

Edward Cooper didn't commit bigamy due to religion (his Idaho State Penitentiary record lists his religion as Catholic). Rather, it seems his decision to marry while still married to another was based, at least in part, on greed. Perhaps he had grown bored with family life in Utah and set out to find something he thought would be better. This seems to have been the case for Harry McJunkin. In January 1937, McJunkin married a young woman from Oregon whom he'd known for "only about two or three weeks." After such a short time, there was certainly much the woman didn't know about her new husband. One of these things was that he was already married; his wife lived in Colorado with their small child. At any rate, her marriage to McJunkin was short-lived. McJunkin, it seems, had a change of heart. He left his new wife in Jerome and sent her a letter instructing her "to forget about him." Then he posted another letter, this one to his first wife in Colorado, proclaiming his love for her and their child. The courts caught up with McJunkin before he could get back to Colorado. He pleaded guilty to bigamy and was sentenced to eighteen months to three years in the penitentiary.

There are few who would disagree that laws against murder, theft, and assault are necessary to ensure safety and protect the population from the abuses of others. Some, however, may disagree about laws aimed at regulating home and family life. Law books, both past and present, are riddled with statutes passed in order to police what many consider personal activities of questionable morality. What, though, is considered "questionable morality"?

In 1873, Congress passed the Comstock Act, which prohibited publishing, distributing, and possessing information of an "obscene, lewd, or lascivious" nature. This included information about contraception and sexual education.[234] As American culture changed and evolved, so did the laws around obscenity. In the 1970s, the Supreme Court established the Miller test, a method for determining obscenity. Materials that fit the following standards "may be considered obscene":

> *1. Whether the average person, applying contemporary adult community standards, finds that the matter, taken as a whole, appeals to prurient interests (i.e., an erotic, lascivious, abnormal, unhealthy, degrading, shameful, or morbid interest in nudity, sex, or excretion);*

> *2. Whether the average person, applying contemporary adult community standards, finds that the matter depicts or describes sexual conduct in a patently offensive way (i.e., ultimate sexual acts, normal or perverted, actual or simulated, masturbation, excretory functions, lewd exhibition of the genitals, or sado-masochistic sexual abuse); and*

> *3. Whether a reasonable person finds that the matter, taken as a whole, lacks serious literary, artistic, political, or scientific value.*[235]

A standard test for obscenity could certainly help determine what materials should be subject to laws and prohibitions, but the issue with the Miller test is its incredible subjectivity. Opinions may differ wildly on whether a person is "average" or "reasonable" or what "contemporary adult community standards" exist. Further, various audiences—based on cultural background, personal history, religious belief, and a plethora of other reasons—will also likely disagree on what may be considered "offensive" or how to define "literary, artistic, political, or scientific value."

What may be considered obscene, lewd, or lascivious also changes over time as cultures evolve. In 1891, Mike Kirby was arrested in Boise for sending an "obscene letter" through the mail to a woman in Owyhee County. Sending the "most disgustingly worded letter" earned Kirby three years of hard labor in the Idaho Penitentiary. Just a year later, a young man named James Clark was sentenced to eighteen months in the penitentiary for the same crime. We have no way of knowing today what the men wrote in the letters, why their recipients had found them so offensive or if "the average person" would find them appealing to "prurient interests." Perhaps the content of the letters accounts for the large difference in the men's sentences. There may have been another factor in play at sentencing, though. Oregon-born James Clark was blue-eyed and light-skinned. Mike Kirby, on the other hand, hailed from the Sandwich Islands in the far south Atlantic and had a dark complexion, dark hair, and "black" eyes. Racism and xenophobia, it seems, played as

The stone yard at the Old Idaho State Penitentiary. Mike Kirby was sentenced to hard labor in the penitentiary for sending an "obscene letter" through the mail. *P1968-57-55, "Idaho State Penitentiary Stone Yard," Idaho State Archives.*

large—perhaps larger—a part in how their crimes were perceived as did the actual words they had written.[236]

Even without knowing the contents, anyone who spends even a short amount of time on social media or the internet may safely conclude that today Kirby and Clark would likely receive no penitentiary time for writing their scandalous letters. Cultural evolution and social progression have turned their transgression from a criminal act into what many may now consider a tasteless and unwelcome action. The passage of time and changing societal expectations and understanding may also change the way that the "contemporary," "average," and "reasonable person" views other Idaho laws and the "criminals" who broke them.

Idaho Statute 18-6601 was written into current state code in 1972. According to this law, "a married man who has sexual intercourse with a woman not his wife, an unmarried man who has sexual intercourse with a married woman, a married woman who has sexual intercourse with a man not her husband, and an unmarried woman who has sexual intercourse with a married man, shall be guilty of adultery." The punishment for such a crime: imprisonment for a period of three months to three years or a fine up to $1,000.[237] Although adultery is technically still a felony in Idaho, it is rarely, if ever, punished. No statewide data set reports figures on adultery charges, and the crime is not included in the annual report filed by the Idaho State Police. However, this was not the case in the late nineteenth and early twentieth centuries in Idaho. Like the laws against bigamy and polygamy, the law prohibiting adultery was initially another way to legally punish Mormons. For those outside of the LDS Church, the crime was prosecuted to hold wayward spouses to account for their behavior and uphold and preserve traditional family values. Whether prosecuted adultery cases always did justice to this purpose, though, is a matter of debate.

Anna Turpin was about thirty years old when she asked an old family friend in Star—a small community just west of Boise—for a job in return for room and board for herself and a man she claimed was her husband. Although the friend in question, Mr. J.F. Ayres, hadn't seen Turpin for many years, he'd known her parents and was happy to oblige. Turpin and her male companion, Fred Law, were hard workers. Law's assistance at Ayres's gristmill was so valuable that Ayres began paying him regular wages in addition to boarding the couple. He had no reason to doubt their sincerity or the veracity of their story.[238]

This idyllic arrangement did not last long. Ayres was surprised when the authorities came and arrested Turpin and Law for adultery. The evidence against them was solid. After all, the two had been caught cohabiting, and prosecutors showed that she was legally married not to Fred Law, but rather to a man named George Turpin. The young lovers pleaded guilty and fell on the mercy of the court.[239]

The couple's defense attorney painted a sympathetic picture. Mrs. Turpin, he shared, was much abused by her "inhuman" husband. Turpin forced his wife to "live a life of shame." The poor woman found love in the arms of Fred Law, "who loved her and who made her happy" and helped her to run away from her miserable marriage. Her husband had caught them once. Anna had refused to return with him, and in the foray that followed, Law shot George in the jaw. The wound rendered him totally deaf. Anna and Law had fled again, this time to Star and Ayres's place. A woman Anna Turpin had thought was her friend betrayed them, ending their peace. Surely, the defense attorney concluded, the "extreme penalties" usually placed on adulterers did not apply in this case. The judge seemed to agree. The law, he believed, was written to punish "men and women who are guilty of a long series of adulterous conduct." Anna Turpin and Fred Law did not fall into that category. Still, their actions had been illegal. Anna was

Fred Law was sentenced to seven months in the Idaho State Penitentiary after being convicted of polygamy with Anna Turpin. Anna was sentenced to five months in the Ada County Jail. *Idaho State Archives.*

sentenced to five months in the Ada County Jail. Law's sentence, probably due to his shooting George Turpin, was tougher. He was given seven months in the Idaho State Penitentiary. Had justice been served? George Turpin, who lost his wife and his full ability to hear, probably didn't think so. However, Anna Turpin and Fred Law—who lost their freedom, their reputations, and their happy and loving life together—most likely didn't either. In this case, the law that was meant to preserve a peaceful and happy home did the opposite.[240]

Laws against bigamy, polygamy and adultery are just part of America's "long history of regulating sexual activity inside marriage." A particular law still on the books in Idaho, though, was originally written and passed to protect the sanctity of marriage by preventing sex outside of its bounds. Statute 18-6605, Idaho's "infamous crime against nature" law, prohibits anal and oral sex, including consensual activity. Added to code in 1972, the law was originally written when Idaho was still a territory. Sexual activity, drafters of the law believed, should be relegated to marital relations and, specifically, procreation.[241]

The law, though, was used to damaging effect when utilized to prosecute homosexuality. Idahoans quickly discerned that the law could be used to punish this "deviant" behavior. In 1919, E.E. Gillespie was accused of committing the "infamous crime against nature" for allegedly engaging in a sex act with another man. He was acquitted, but the accusation and trial cemented his reputation in the community. One year later, Gillespie was arrested for same offense again. This time, another man was accused with him. W.E. Danner stood trial with Gillespie for, as the *Idaho Statesman* reported, "committing a statutory offense." A witness, by peering through a tiny screw hole in the floor, had seen the two carrying out the act in the room below. Danner claimed mistaken identity—a plausible defense considering the witness's questionable vantage point. The jury, though, did not believe him. Danner's co-defendant was already a suspected homosexual, a suggestion that seemed enough to cement both their fates. Gillespie and Danner were found guilty of the "infamous crime against nature" and sentenced to five and a half years in the Idaho State Penitentiary. Danner "was unable to stand the strain" at sentencing; "his eyes filled with tears, and his body shook with muffled sobs." Gillespie remained composed and "conduct[ed] himself stoically." Ultimately, Danner served a year and a half, while Gillespie served two and a half.[242]

Danner and Gillespie were certainly not the only men in Boise to be convicted of the "infamous crime against nature" in response to homosexual activity, whether actual or admitted. On March 29, 1959, Boise police investigated a car parked behind a nightclub in downtown Boise. The passenger, they reported, looked obviously intoxicated. What police claimed to find were two men engaging in a sexual act. The men, Howard Roller and Denny Denton, were both arrested. Roller pleaded guilty. He was a homosexual, he said, and had invited Denny into his car for the purposes of sex. Roller was sentenced to six months in the Ada County Jail. Denton proclaimed his innocence. He was not gay, he said, and had been married to a woman as recently as two years before. Denton testified that he had been intoxicated when Roller invited him into the car for another drink. The jury deliberated for just an hour before finding Denton guilty. He was sentenced to no more than five years in the Idaho State Penitentiary and was paroled in 1962. The discrepancy in Roller's and Denton's sentences is striking.

Perhaps Roller was given a shorter sentence in county jail, in comparison to Denton's longer term in the penitentiary, because he'd admitted guilt. Denton had a criminal record. He'd been previously convicted of forging a check and had violated his parole several times. Additionally, Denton was of Puerto Rican descent; his parents had been immigrants. The idea that racism and xenophobia may have played into Denton's conviction cannot be discounted.[243]

Racism, xenophobia, homophobia, and a general mistrust of anyone "different" was running rampant through the United States in the middle of the twentieth century. Americans had emerged from World War II victorious, and the societal changes that followed made them suspicious. After the war, American demographics shifted. Young people left their rural homes, sometimes for the first time in generations, and poured into cities to take advantage of the many new work opportunities that had arisen. In the anonymity of these crowded spaces, people of all ages felt free to embrace feelings and beliefs that had previously been frowned upon, restricted, or prohibited. The pursuit of same-sex relationships became, for many, a reality where before it had seemed an impossibility. More and conservative Americans believed, like their Victorian ancestors, that traditional ways of life and the sanctity of marriage and family were under attack.

The Lavender Scare grew out of these fears. In the 1950s and '60s, Americans, specifically those searching for employment or advancement within government agencies, were subjected to interview questions that most of us have likely never faced. Individuals were asked pointedly about their sexuality, whether they'd ever experienced homosexual feelings or engaged in homosexual activity. The Lavender Scare grew out of this irrational fear of homosexuality. According to popular opinion and contemporary psychology, homosexuality was a mental illness.

This anti-homosexual conduct went so far as to label same-sex relations a threat the United States on the same level as communism. Senator Joseph McCarthy, infamous for his anti-communist rhetoric and extremism, believed that homosexuals were "susceptible to Communist recruitment" due to their "peculiar mental twists." McCarthy's rhetoric linked communists and homosexuals in many ways. Both groups were "morally weak or psychologically disturbed." They were "godless" and "undermined the traditional family" by actively recruiting others into their "secret subculture." Homosexuals, McCarthy and his supporters believed, were a threat to national security. Laws were created throughout the United States to root out suspected homosexual behavior.[244]

Idaho's "infamous crime against nature" law was utilized in force in the 1950s. In 1955, Boise was rocked by possibly the biggest scandal in its history. That fall, three men were arrested for engaging in sexual relations with teenage boys. The men arrested were not who the community might have expected. They included relatively well-known men in town from local families. Their arrests were only the beginning, though. The investigation meant to "crush the monster" dug deep into Boise society. More men were arrested for relations with teenage boys, but the majority of the hundreds of men questioned and the sixteen charged were guilty only of same-sex acts with consenting adults. For most of them, the "mere perception that one is gay" was enough to ruin his life. One of the accused, the vice-president of a Boise bank, recalled that he pleaded guilty because it was his only option due to "all the publicity and stink that had been raised." His life, he said, "was ruined anyway."[245] The scandal left hundreds of lives—those of the accused, their families, the accusers, and any others associated—scarred for years, sometimes irreparably.*

The United States was founded on the principal of "liberty and justice for all." Perhaps, though, there are times when the laws aren't quite just—times where they are written in an effort to oppress a particular group of people, are subjective in nature or are applied unevenly. There are other laws that most, if not all, would agree are essential for a peaceful society—laws against theft, murder, and assault. Sometimes, though, the reasons for why the crime is committed can call the idea of justice into question.

PATRIARCHAL VALUES AND UNCLEAR INTENTIONS

Much of the American legal system, including laws and statutes, are based on English common law. The doctrine of coverture was one of those Anglo-Saxon inheritances. According to coverture, a woman was legally considered her husband's possession. A woman did have the right to properties she'd brought into the marriage but was unable to conduct any legal business with them without her husband. She did not even have the right to remain sole guardian over her children in the event of his death. A woman's whole legal identity belonged to her husband. She was dependent

---

* The 1955 Boise homosexual scandal deserves a much more in-depth discussion than what is included here. John Gerassi's 1966 book, *The Boys of Boise*, and *The Fall of '55*, a documentary by Seth Randal, are comprehensive sources on this dark event in the city's history.

on him in nearly every way. This began to change in 1848 with the passage of the Married Women's Property Act in New York. This allowed her to "enter contracts on her own" and "collect rents or receive an inheritance in her own right." The act also stipulated that women were not liable for their husband's debts and could file lawsuits on their own behalf. By 1900, all other states had passed similar laws. In 1896, six years after statehood, Idaho gave women the right to vote, a full twenty-four years before the United States would ratify the Nineteenth Amendment, offering that right to all women.* This was another giant step in granting women the same rights and privileges that men held.[246]

Despite these advances in equality, women still had a long way to go before they held the same rights as their male counterparts. Prior to 1960, women were still unable to open bank accounts on their own, and it wasn't until the 1974 Equal Credit Opportunity Act that women could have credit cards without their husband's signature (unmarried women often were unable to have a credit card at all). The Fair Labor Standards Act, passed in 1938, established a federal minimum wage, which cut down on pay differences between men and women in many jobs. However, pay inequality still exists. In 2020, women earned, on average, $0.84 to each $1.00 earned by men, and women remain "overrepresented in lower-paying occupations relative to their share of the workforce." Domestic factors are one of the leading causes of this issue. Women are more likely to be the primary caregivers, meaning they have fewer opportunities for attaining education, have more and longer employment gaps, and miss more days of work due to caregiver issues. All of this adds to up women often getting passed over for positions or promotions that go to men.[247]

Through the middle of the twentieth century, dozens of Idaho women were convicted of economic crimes like forgery or passing bad checks. Mary Margaret Klingensmith spent almost eleven months in the Idaho State Penitentiary in 1953 after issuing a check without funds at a Boise grocery store. Klingensmith, thirty-three, had reportedly asked the grocery owner not to deposit the ten-dollar check until she returned with cash. She was arrested before she was able to do so. Following her time in the penitentiary, Klingensmith asked for and was granted a divorce. Was her husband's

---

* After the Fourteenth Amendment was passed in 1868 granting Black Americans the right to vote, systemic and overt acts of racism hindered their efforts to do so. Native Americans did not receive voting rights until 1924 with the passage of the Snyder Act. Even then, it still took nearly half a century for all states to allow indigenous peoples the right to vote. Unfortunately, voting rights remain a contentious issue in the United States today, and many minority groups are still fighting for equal access to voting opportunities.

inability to support her the reason Klingensmith had both committed her crime and asked for a divorce?[248]

Just on the heels of Mary Klingensmith's arrest and conviction, twenty-five-year-old Elda Lennon was also arrested in Boise for passing bad checks. She had written five different checks, each for thirty dollars, in Boise groceries. Although authorities suspected that Lennon's husband had forced her into writing the bad checks, she was nonetheless convicted and sentenced to spend time in the Idaho State Penitentiary. She was released after almost a year and half.* Were Klingensmith's and Lennon's crimes committed out of greed or circumstance? The relatively small amounts, along with the fact the checks were passed in grocery stores, points more in the direction of the latter.[249]

The conditions surrounding the case of young Mary Mills lend themselves even more to the idea of crime as an outcome of limited circumstances. Mary grew up in Gooding, Idaho, with her parents and younger brother. At some point in her youth, Mary spent time at the Idaho Industrial School, a facility for wayward youth. When she was there is unclear, but it may have been when she was between sixteen and eighteen years old. In 1932, when Mary was sixteen, her father died suddenly, leaving her mother to support Mary and her twelve-year-old brother. In 1934 or 1935, Mary began living in Emmett alone. Perhaps Mary had been sent to the Industrial School following her father's death.[250]

Life in Emmett was not easy for Mary. By the fall of 1935, she had made her way to Boise, probably hoping to improve her situation. In Boise, Mary lived with "various men" who were "all of a rather low moral character, who frequent the night clubs." Mary depended on those men, it seems, as "she had no apparant [sic] means of livelihood while in this county." After her first few months in town, Mary's name began to come up in public health investigations. Doctors treating men for venereal disease reported Mary to the health department as a contact. Authorities had Mary arrested and held on a vagrancy charge while an investigation was conducted. Rather than put her in jail, authorities decided that the best thing for Mary was to "provide some means of treating and caring for her." Mary was returned to Emmett, and the Gem County Health Department in Emmett was charged with her care and treatment. Mary didn't stay in Emmett for long, though. By December, she was back in Boise, living with one of the men she'd been connected to before. Ada County authorities again arrested Mary and

---

* Accounting for inflation, Klingensmith's $10 check would be worth approximately $102 today. Lennon's fraudulent transactions were worth more—approximately $1,500.

Mary Margaret Klingensmith and Elda Lennon were sentenced to time in the Idaho State Penitentiary for crimes of check fraud. They were just two of the several women who served time in the Women's Ward for similar crimes. *P1984-15-33, "Idaho State Penitentiary Women's Ward," Idaho State Archives.*

this time charged her with exposing another person to the infection of a dangerous disease.[251]

Despite the Ada County's prosecuting attorney's judgement that Mary had "no criminal tendency," he still wrote that he believed she was "a menace to society." Mary had "no moral standards whatsoever," and although she should know right from wrong, she had "no regard as to spreading her disease or of sexual conversation with anyone." Mary, just nineteen, was convicted and sentenced to one to two years in the Idaho State Penitentiary. The prosecutor recommended that once she was released, Mary should "probably be committed to a Feeble Minded Institute," as she was "of very low intelligence."[252]

Mary Mill's booking photo shows a very young women, her youthful face round and wrinkle-free but spotted with sores, scars, or bruises. She wears a low-cut, sleeveless dress, shiny like silk or satin, and a butterfly clip adorns hair

Nineteen-year-old Mary Mills in her Idaho State Penitentiary booking photo. Her satin dress and uncertain expression imply a young woman confused and possibly scared about her current situation. *AR42, Idaho State Penitentiary Collection, "Inmate 5231, Mary Mills," Idaho State Archives.*

that looks unwashed and unkempt. Her face holds little expression—perhaps a just bit of confusion and uncertainty.[253] Everything about Mary's story—the death of her father; her time in the reform school; showing up in another part of the state alone and without prospects; her mature, attention-seeking dress—suggests that Mary was, like so many other nineteen-year-old women, trying desperately to find her place in the world and way to survive on her own. Mary's real crime had been that she was poor and uneducated and had no support system. She had been doing what she needed to survive. The wrongs she had committed were an unfortunate byproduct of her desperation.*

Lottie Ashdown may also have been feeling some desperation on March 21, 1949, when she bought a hamburger from a roadside stand and laced it with strychnine before giving it to her husband. Lottie married Vivian Ashdown in 1928, and the couple had three daughters. The marriage lasted nearly twenty years before the pair divorced in 1947. One year later, in October 1948, Lottie remarried to a man named Lacey following a brief three-month affair. This new union, though, was as fleeting as the courtship. By March 19, 1949, the two had divorced, and Lottie and Vivian were standing before the Canyon County justice of the peace to be married again.[254]

---

* Mary Mills was granted parole in 1936 after serving eleven months. In her letter to the parole board, Mary wrote that she intended to return home to care for her mother and "large family." She promised to "lead a moral and industrious life." Mary did not return to her family, as by 1940, her mother and brother were living in Los Angeles. Rather, Mary moved to Twin Falls and became a bookkeeper and was married twice. She had no other run-ins with the law.

Two days after their second wedding, Lottie gave her husband the poisoned hamburger as he drove the two of them from Nampa to the family ranch. Strychnine is a white and odorless but bitter-tasting powder that can cause serious illness and death in even small doses. Within minutes of ingesting the tainted burger, Vivian Ashdown would have experienced painful muscle spasms and rigidity in his limbs. His jaw may have tightened and even locked as his neck and back arched uncontrollably. Quickly, he would have lost the ability to breathe. His death was certainly painful and probably terrifying. The whole ordeal would have been as horrific to witness.[255]

As her husband shuddered, spasmed, and then slumped in the driver's seat, Lottie took the wheel. When she reached the Ashdown ranch, she later testified, she felt for Vivian's pulse. Finding none, she drove directly to the local doctor. Dr. Kelly, based in Homedale in Owyhee County, was a small-town physician. His patients' primary complaints generally consisted of minor illnesses, injuries from farm accidents, or other routine ailments. The circumstances surrounding Vivian Ashdown's death raised his suspicions. Dr. Kelly called in a Boise pathologist to help with an autopsy. The lethal amounts of strychnine found in Vivian's stomach indicated his death was not due to a mysterious ailment or an unfortunate accident.[256]

Although strychnine is now almost exclusively used as a pesticide, it used to be synthesized into medications. The compound's stimulant effects were used to treat heart and lung issues. As a medication, strychnine could be purchased over the counter. In the course of investigating the incident, officials discovered that a "Mrs. Jack Brown" had purchased strychnine from a drugstore in Caldwell on March 12, more than a week before Vivian Ashdown's death. When questioned, the pharmacist identified Lottie Ashdown as Mrs. Jack Brown. Lottie was arrested in Salt Lake City, where she'd traveled for her husband's interment.[257]

Lottie did not deny her involvement in Vivian's death. She was "pale but calm" in the courtroom and pleaded guilty to first-degree murder. Was Lottie aware, the judge asked, that the punishment for such a crime may be life in prison or death by hanging? "With a slight tremor in her voice," the woman indicated that she was. Her plea, she also agreed, had been made without pressure or promise of leniency. She spoke calmly as she explained the reasons behind her actions to the court. Lottie had killed her husband, she said, to protect her three daughters. Her actions were necessary for her girls' "peace and happiness." Lottie escaped a death sentence and was sentenced to life in prison. She was released on parole after serving thirteen and a half years.[258]

Though known as Lottie Ashdown in the newspapers, she was booked in the Idaho State Penitentiary under her legal name: Elizabeth Lacey. She appears older than her thirty-seven years, and a scar—evidence of her husband's domestic abuse—is visible above her collar. *AR42, Idaho State Penitentiary Collection, "Inmate 7610, Elizabeth Lottie Lacey," Idaho State Archives.*

Lottie Ashdown knew or suspected that her husband was mistreating their daughters, and nearly any mother with that knowledge would do whatever necessary to protect her children. There is no evidence to support Lottie's claims, but her Idaho State Penitentiary booking photo provides a clue as to how unhappy and violent life in the Ashdown household may have been.[259] The photo shows a stoic woman; Lottie stares straight ahead, her face betraying no emotion. Her dark hair, pulled up in pins in a style prevalent at the time, is streaked with gray. Her face looks older than its thirty-seven years. A scar is visible above her white collar. The thin, faint line runs across the width of her neck, evidence of Vivian Ashdown's attempt to cut her throat.[260]

There is much about Lottie Ashdown's life that we don't know. Why did she marry and divorce Mr. Lacey so suddenly? Why did she choose to remarry a man she most certainly already knew to be abusive, especially if, as the timing of the poison purchase suggests, she'd already decided to kill him? Did contemporary laws limiting women's economic power force Lottie to do the unthinkable? Was Lottie Ashdown acting with villainous intention, or were her decisions made out of desperation?

Although some clues allow speculation, Lottie Ashdown's actual motivations may never be known. Alta McGee's intentions are even more unclear. McGee and her husband, John, had a tumultuous relationship. John McGee was a bartender and, according to his wife, a swindler. On at least two occasions, Alta testified, John had tried to enlist her assistance in blackmailing other men for money. One of the schemes involved having Alta invite a man to the McGee house. Alta was to entertain the man in the parlor alone. John would then burst into the room and catch the man "alienating the affection of his wife." John's plan was to tell the man he would drop the matter for a sum of money. In another instance, John planned to tell a man visiting from Spokane that he would inform the man's wife that he had been "attentive to Mrs. McGee" while visiting Boise—unless, of course, the visitor paid up.[261]

According to Alta, she "absolutely refused to have anything to do with such a scheme." Further, she claimed, her husband was neglectful; he failed to buy her any clothing "except for a pair of slippers." The man from Spokane was a good friend, Alta reported. He'd provided her not only with the clothing her husband had not but also food and fuel to get her through winter and $100 in cash. The two had a photograph taken together during his visit, Alta said—a photograph that her husband had threatened to mail to her friend's wife if he wasn't paid.[262]

Perhaps John McGee's extortion threats were the machinations of a jealous husband. Maybe John knew that Alta and her "friend" were closer than she let on. It's also possible that he was resentful that another man was providing for his wife when he either would or could not. Alta may seem a sympathetic character. However, she told these stories of her husband's misdeeds while defending herself in court against charges that she'd assaulted him with a deadly weapon. Alta, according to her own testimony, had grown tired of her husband's womanizing ways.[263]

On the evening of May 4, 1908, Alta witnessed her husband driving a carriage up and down the street outside her home with another woman. The pair were trying to "tantalize" her, Alta claimed. Enraged, she had a friend of hers bring another carriage around, and she followed after John and his companion, a revolver at her side. She caught up with them outside of a saloon on Main Street, where John hurled insults at his wife. Alta responded by firing three shots at him and the woman he was with.[264]

Alta showed no remorse as she testified. On the contrary, she admitted that "she might have regretted it had she hit McGee when he was alone," but if she'd hit both him and the other woman, which was her admitted intent, "she would not have cared much." They were both "looking for trouble," Alta claimed. The other woman, Alta continued, had called her and told her she'd be out riding with John. At that point, Alta said, she determined that she would "shoot them if [she] caught them."[265]

The "drive-by shooting" was also not the first run-in Alta had had with one of her husband's alleged paramours, and the alleged blackmail was not the only trouble for which John was responsible. Earlier in the couple's troubled relationship, Alta had horsewhipped a young woman that she'd seen out driving with her husband. According to others' testimony, John was often outside Alta's home (the couple was no longer living together at the time of the incident), "prowling around…nearly every night…and bothering her." Just a week before the shooting, Alta and a friend had been driving down Main Street to a funeral. John, standing in front of a saloon, saw them go by, "laughed ridiculously…and called them all a vile name."[266]

The McGees' marriage was obviously toxic and unhealthy, and Alta's actions and unrepentant attitude shouldn't be condoned. However, both of the McGees hold some responsibility for what happened on May 4, 1908, in front of a saloon on Boise's Main Street. Public opinion was that the "womanizer had gotten pretty much what he deserved." The jury seemed to agree. They found Alta guilty of assault with intent to commit murder but recommended the judge show mercy. She received ten months in the Idaho State Penitentiary and served just three months before the governor granted her clemency. John faced no legal consequences. The two were divorced almost immediately, and in 1909, Alta married again and appears to have lived out her days quietly.[267]

Women like Mary Klingensmith, Elda Lennon, Mary Mills, Lottie Ashdown and Alta McGee all depended on the men in their lives for support and survival. When those men let them down, each of those women faced the consequences. Some, like Mills, bore no ill will toward anyone. They didn't intend to purposely injure or harm anyone, but simply did what was necessary to survive. Others, like Ashdown and McGee, each for her own reason, felt such a level of desperation that they took drastic measures, sometimes with intended deadly consequences. Ashdown felt the need to protect herself and her daughters; McGee wanted the man who'd vowed to care for and protect her to show her respect and let her live in peace. While their actions can in no way be condoned, perhaps, presented in the correct context, they may be understood.

At other times, though, a crime is so heinous and the culprit so unrepentant that it renders any possible defensible motive completely trivial.

Widow with a "Heart of Stone"

Twenty-one-year-old Jennie Daley glared at prosecutors from the witness stand.* She had acted purely in self-defense, she claimed, on October 6, 1904—the night her husband was murdered. Charles Daley was threatening his young wife and had been for some time. Because of these threats, Mrs. Daley had rented a revolver from a local hardware store for fifty cents. On the night in question, she carried it concealed at her side. When Mr. Daley began to move toward her "with a threat on his lips," Mrs. Daley drew and shot him in the head two times.[268]

Did Mrs. Daley call the authorities? The prosecutors pressed the woman for more details. Her answers were "surly, half defiant."[269] No, she hadn't, Mrs. Daley reported. Instead, "with incomprehensible heartlessness," she'd covered her suffering husband with a blanket and tried to sleep. About three hours later, though, the seriously wounded Mr. Daley began to moan and stir. He tried to stand, Mrs. Daley testified, and again threatened her life. She grabbed a hatchet from the floor and "beat him over the head." Then, to be certain he was dead, the woman pushed her revolver into her mortally wounded husband's chest, as close as she could tell to his heart, and pulled the trigger again. Then she pulled the blanket back over the body and went to bed.[270]

Jennie Daley's confession was lurid and sensational, but it didn't stand long. Investigators continued to press the woman, and under cross-examination, she crumbled. She had rented the revolver, yes, Mrs. Daley confirmed, but had not pulled the trigger. That deed had been done by her lover, Fred Bond.[271]

Bond, a slightly built man in his mid-thirties, was a miner by trade. He'd recently arrived in Boise from Mackey, in northeastern Idaho, and was renting a room from the Daleys in their home at 414 North Third Street.

---

* The *Idaho Statesman* spelled Daley as "Daly" in all its coverage of this crime. Official records utilize the "Daley" spelling, which is used here.

He and young Mrs. Daley, it seems, took to each other almost immediately. Mrs. Daley admitted that she was infatuated with Bond and "declared he was equally in love with her." The pair spent a great deal of time together, so much so that Mr. Daley, a few weeks before his murder, had ordered Bond to leave his home after the other man had "boldly confessed his love for Mrs. Daley." Bond left begrudgingly but returned two weeks later at Mrs. Daley's insistence.[272]

Charles Daley's murder, Mrs. Daley now proclaimed, was all Fred Bond's fault. Bond had suggested she rent the revolver. He had pressured her to pick a fight with her husband and use that opportunity to shoot him in self-defense. Mrs. Daley testified her husband had returned home on the night in question in high spirits. He found his wife in Bond's company in his parlor but was still "cheerful and good natured." Mr. Daley mentioned plans to attend the theater, Mrs. Daley related, but she told him that she "did not care to go" and "no longer took any pleasure in her husband's company." Instead of growing angry, her husband had seemed weary and resigned. Mrs. Daley recounted the exchange that followed.

"Jennie, do you love Fred?" Mr. Daley had asked.

"I do," she'd replied.

Mr. Daley looked to Bond for confirmation, which was immediately given. "Then it's all over between me and wife," he reportedly said. Then he bent to put his shoes back on.[273]

The argument Jennie had been waiting for never commenced, and she was unable to follow through on Bond's lethal directive. Instead, she went into the kitchen, followed by her lover. She pleaded with Bond to reconsider, but he was set on murder. He took the gun from her, stalked back to the parlor, and fired two shots into Mr. Daley's head. The rest of the evening's events, Mrs. Daley testified, played out much like she'd said in her first statement, except that it was Bond, not herself, who bludgeoned Mr. Daley and then shot him again. Bond had not only "suggested" Daley's murder but had also "performed the atrocious deed without her assistance." As for Bond, he firmly denied his part in the event. His answers were "snappy and shifty," and he rarely gave a direct reply and wasted no words." He had nothing to say in reply to Mrs. Daley's statement except that he was "an innocent man, that's all." Both Mrs. Daley and Bond were arrested for murder.[274]

The pair handled their arrests and the accusations against them very differently. Bond, the *Idaho Statesman* reported, lost his "nonchalant air" and began to show evidence of strain. Despite his "ravenous" appetite, he seemed to grow thinner by the day. His eyes "receded into his head," and "he is actually turning green," the *Stateman* reporter wrote with barely disguised enthusiasm. Bond's previously round and full face looked shrunken, and his complexion was sallow. He was "morose, taciturn, and nervous, his braggadocio having entirely disappeared." Despite his steadfast denial of involvement in Mr. Daley's murder, Bond seemed a man full of worry and despair.[275]

Mrs. Daley, on the other hand, appeared almost entirely emotionally unaffected by all that had transpired. At her husband's funeral, she shed a few quiet tears, but "in less than five minutes she was her indifferent self again." Police admitted her into her home to gather the necessities she would need in jail, but "for all the emotion she displayed…she might have been selecting clothing for a pleasant journey."[276] At her preliminary hearing, held just a little more than a week after the murder, Mrs. Daley played the part of grieving widow, sitting quietly, dressed in a large-brimmed, black hat and matching veil. However, as the coroner described Mr. Daley's body—"short, thick set…with a bald head"—she burst into laughter. Her stoicism returned quickly, though. She took the news that she would be tried for first-degree murder "without as much as a quiver."[277]

Mrs. Daley and Bond were scheduled for separate murder trials. Bond's came first, and Mrs. Daley was the star witness. More than two hundred witnesses, mostly women, gathered to hear the sordid details. The women "swarmed behind the railing, appropriated the seats reserved for attorneys, encroached on the clerk's desk, and emptied the water pitchers provided for counsel." Some brought their infants with them, and the children's cries periodically broke through the proceedings. Most of these women were certainly young, married, and mothers to young children. They were not wealthy but solidly middle class, married to men with stable jobs. Mrs. Daley could have been any one of them. Perhaps they all felt the need to hear her story. Maybe they were trying to determine how a woman just like them had ended up here—testifying against her lover and soon facing her own trial as an accomplice for the gruesome murder of her own husband. What had gone wrong in Mrs. Daley's life, and could those same things happen to them?[278]

If those women were there to hear the scandalous and salacious details of the crime, Mrs. Daley's testimony did not let them down. Her behavior was more subdued than it had been directly following her arrest. Mrs. Daley still wore the black of mourning, and her feet hung six inches off the floor as she sat in the high witness chair. She was pale and spoke with no emotion and so softly that the judge often had to ask her to speak up. Overall, Mrs.

Jennie Daley claimed that her lover, Fred Bond, was solely responsible for her husband's murder. In the courtroom, she showed little remorse or sadness over his death. *AR42, Idaho State Penitentiary Collection, "Inmate 1096, Jennie Daley," Idaho State Archives.*

Daley cut "a pitiful figure on the stand." Bond's lawyer, who was trying to prove that her story had too many holes to be true, repeatedly caught her contradicting herself. He asked several questions that ended with "did you not?" Mrs. Daley would answer in the affirmative, but in her replies she "frequently contradicted herself." Was Mrs. Daley confused by the phrasing or was she purposefully misleading? A reporter for the *Idaho Statesman* struck a sympathetic tone. "That she is easily influenced was shown repeatedly in her answers to questions," he wrote. She "appeared absolutely helpless on minor points." Despite the defense's intense questioning and her often inconsistent answers, Mrs. Daley never wavered on the important points of the story. Bond had devised the plan, fired the shots that struck Mr. Daley in the head, bludgeoned the poor man with the hatchet, and pulled the trigger again to ensure that her husband was dead. She was "questioned…without mercy" but could not be confused "on vital matters."[279]

Why, Bond's defense questioned, had Mrs. Daley confessed at first if Bond had been the perpetrator all along? That, Mrs. Daley answered, was also Bond's idea. After he'd murdered her husband, Bond had told Mrs. Daley to turn herself in for the crime. If she claimed self-defense, Bond had told her, she would "probably escape punishment." The same would not be true if he were to confess. She agreed to keep them both from prison.[280]

When Mrs. Daley took the stand again the next day to continue her examination, she was still stoic and unemotional but much more composed and confident. She was "prompt and to the point" as she repeated her story, never wavering from the account she'd given the day before. A separate line of questioning was added, though. Why, the judge wanted to know, had Mrs. Daley recanted her first confession? Her answer here was also quick and concise. She was not intimidated or afraid, she said, but rather was concerned about her daughter, two-year-old Charlotte, and the "disgrace which her first confession would bring upon the little girl." Others had also counseled her to tell the truth, including a member of the jury at the coroner's inquest, a friend of hers who "knew she was incapable of killing her husband," and the deputy county attorney, who, with his wife, was watching Charlotte while Mrs. Daley was in jail. Mrs. Daley may not have been intimidated into recanting, but she had certainly been influenced.[281]

Bond was quiet during Mrs. Daley's testimony. He did not so much as shake his head to agree or disagree with any of her statements. The only time he showed any interest or emotion throughout the proceedings was when witnesses testified to seeing the two together in public. After deliberating for just over three hours, the jury returned a verdict: guilty of murder in the first degree. Bond reacted to the verdict as stoically as he had the rest of the trial. His anxiety was only given away by his fingers fumbling with his hat. Bond was again fumbling nervously with his hat when the judge sentenced him to hang for his crime. Prison guards reported that after they'd placed him in his cell on death row, Bond sat quietly smoking a cigar, "legs crossed and his gaze fixed on nothing." Neither the verdict nor the sentence seemed an outward shock to him.[282]

Compared to the spectacle of Bond's trial, Mrs. Daley's was quiet. The public, including the women of Boise who'd taken such an interest, had heard her story. The main culprit had been convicted of the crime, and the public seems to have made up their minds already as to Mrs. Daley's character. They seemed content to learn of her fate from the papers. The trial was able to move at a rapid pace. Mrs. Daley's defense tried to place the entire blame on Bond. Hardly any new evidence was introduced, however, making it extremely difficult to show that Mrs. Daley was innocent of any involvement in her husband's murder.[283]

The defense changed tactics, though, and tried to make Mrs. Daley as sympathetic a figure as possible. Her attorney relayed the story of Mrs. Daley's sad childhood. She had grown up in St. Louis, never knowing her father and only living with her mother for a few years before she was "sent… out to beg on the streets" before being sent to reform school. Following her time at the school, Mrs. Daley joined the workforce. One of her jobs was for Mr. Daley. She "went to work for Mr. Daly on a Saturday and married him on the following Tuesday." She was nineteen; Mr. Daley was fifty-six. The Daleys had been married three years and had moved to Boise less than a year prior. Mrs. Daley's life, the defense attempted to show, was in a near-constant state of upheaval and turmoil.[284]

Mrs. Daley took the stand in her own defense. She'd married in order to have a stable home, Mrs. Daley testified. She did love Fred Bond, but she also feared him. The man had her under his complete control and had "unduly influenced" her. The prosecutor made Mrs. Daley repeat some of the statements she'd made that implicated her in the murder but did little to refute any of the statements made in her defense. Instead of further implicating Mrs. Daley, a *Statesman* reporter implied, the prosecutor succeeded in showing that she "was really not an accessory but a victim of Bond."[285]

The jury deliberated for ten hours on Mrs. Daley's fate. At closing arguments, the prosecutors laid out the facts of the case, almost all of which were based on the testimony of Mrs. Daley herself. The defense had relied on emotion. Her actions were, the defense said, "based upon [the] young woman's lacking of training and education which…dulled her sense of right and wrong and rendered her an easy victim of the wiles of an unscrupulous man." The jury fell somewhere in between of the two arguments. They found Mrs. Daley guilty of manslaughter, which, by definition, means they believed the crime was not maliciously planned in advance. Yet the judge disagreed. How had the jury come to believe that Mrs. Daley had not acted with "premeditation, malice, or revenge"?[286] However, the judge decreed, the jury had reached a verdict, and it would stand. He sentenced Mrs. Daley to the maximum allowable: ten years in the Idaho State Penitentiary. Despite the sympathy she'd attempted, and sometimes succeeded, to gather at trial, most believed that she "escaped with a very light punishment." Mrs. Daley may well have agreed. She "received her sentence with a smile…fondled her little daughter…chatted with friends and appeared to be delighted at the prospect of a change in quarters." "I will still be a young woman when I get out," she told those gathered around her.[287]

After an unsuccessful appeal, Bond was sentenced to hang on August 10, 1906. "You know what the Bible says: 'Eat, drink, and be merry, for tomorrow we die,'" he told a fellow prisoner at dinner the night before his execution. He ate a large dinner, read his Bible late into the night, and slept soundly in his last twelve hours. On the appointed morning, he "stood untremblingly" and listened as the warden read his death sentence. The two men shook hands, and Bond calmly told all witnesses goodbye. Bond seemed resigned to his fate.[288]

Jennie Daley took in the news of her lover's execution with absolutely no emotion. She seemed "entirely undisturbed" by the whole matter. One of the penitentiary guards reported, "Perhaps there is no convict in the state penitentiary...who has exhibited as little interest and compassion" in Fred Bond's execution than the "widow of the man whom Bond was convicted of killing and the woman who is now serving time for the part she took in the murder." The guards seemed moved by Bond's stoic end, but Mrs. Daley showed neither grief nor remorse.[289]

The "woman with a heart of stone" served six of her ten years before she was paroled. Shortly after her release, Mrs. Daley left Boise and returned to St. Louis to live with her grandmother. A number of members of the Woman's Christian Temperance Union accompanied her, as they'd "interested themselves in her behalf for some time" and had "done everything in their power to give her a chance to lead a new life."[290]

Despite his repeated denials, William H.H. "Fred" Bond was hanged for the murder of Charles Daley. According to contemporary accounts, he was calm and stoic as he went to the gallows. *AR42, Idaho State Penitentiary Collection, "Inmate 1091, Fred Bond," Idaho State Archives.*

Was justice served in Charles Daley's murder? Did contemporary witnesses see Jennie Daley's young age, small stature, and quiet, rough upbringing, slightly confused answers to a tough line of questioning as evidence that she had been used as a man's pawn? The judge and even the prosecutor seemed to show a bit of sympathy toward her. Was it, though, early twentieth-century misogyny that allowed her to escape with a light sentence for the horrendous crime she'd been a party to? Perhaps her behavior and appearance were part of a well-planned and cultivated façade. Was Fred Bond—a rough miner, covetous of another man's wife—solely responsible for the murder? Or was he the pawn in Jennie Daley's game?

True motive is often impossible to pinpoint. After all, what hard evidence can be used to prove an individual's true emotional state, beliefs, and intentions? In the absence of motive, then, is it possible to truly ensure justice?

AND JUSTICE FOR ALL?

*T*n 1994, an eighteen-year-old Idaho man was convicted of sex crimes and forced to register as a sex offender for engaging in consensual sex with a sixteen-year-old boy. A straight man would not have faced the same punishment, as the age of consent in Idaho is sixteen. The basis for the judgment was Idaho's "infamous crime against nature law."[291]

In 2003, the U.S. Supreme Court ruled that laws aimed at banning "private, consensual sex between adults" were unconstitutional. The State of Idaho continued to enforce the law, though. Later that year, a man was required to register as a sex offender in Idaho because nearly two decades earlier, he'd been convicted in a state with its own "crime against nature" law for having consensual oral sex with his wife. The man, identified only as John Doe in court documents, filed suit against the State of Idaho in September 2020. In December, the man convicted in 1994 joined the lawsuit, and in September 2021, a federal judge ruled in their favor. "The state of Idaho," the judge stated, has "no legitimate interest" in enforcing the "infamous crime against nature" law in this manner. Through December 2020, forty-one Idahoans have been required to register as sex offenders after conviction of an "infamous crime against nature," severely limiting where they could live and work. The September 2021 ruling opens up the possibility that others convicted under the law may also seek the means to have their sentences overturned.[292]

One of the goals of the justice system in the United States is to ensure "the fair and impartial administration of justice."[293] But how do we determine what is fair and what is just? Do those concepts mean the same things to everyone, and how do we account for the passage and time and evolution of society, culture, and values?

The western frontier in the mid- to late nineteenth century was in dire need of law, order, and justice. The vigilantes, for many, were the answer to the problems crime was causing in their communities. For others, the vigilantes were a menace—an unchecked group that, in the name of upholding the law, broke several themselves. Laws regulating and prohibiting prostitution were aimed at defending women and protecting the sanctity of home and marriage. But those laws arguably did more harm than good for the women who depended on sex work to survive. Prohibition—the great "Noble Experiment"—was supposed to reduce crime, curb poverty and divorce rates, and lead to a more productive society. Instead, many found themselves unemployed, rates of certain crimes soared, and thousands died or suffered debilitating health issues. Did the laws written to punish immoral behavior have the intended effect, or did their often-ambiguous language lead to questionable convictions? Do such laws really lead to a more ethical and moral society, or do they allow a space for the government to intrude into Americans' private lives? Perhaps the answers to each of these questions lie somewhere in the middle. They sit in the uncomfortable gray space between the clear distinctions of black and white—right and wrong—that most of us prefer. As our communities grow and evolve, we may find that uncomfortable gray bubble growing as we are introduced to new ideas that challenge our preconceived notions of right and wrong, fair and unfair, just and unjust.

Idaho was the fastest-growing state in the nation in 2019–20, with most of that growth happening in the state's cities. The population of Ada County grew 26 percent between 2010 and 2020, and the city of Boise grew almost 15 percent. The growth is projected to continue, and as Boiseans learn to live with their new neighbors, it is only inevitable that we will find ourselves face to face with new ideas and concepts that challenge the ways we perceive what is right, just, and fair. How we respond to those challenges will add another important chapter to the story of Boise's history.[294]

NOTES

Prologue

1. Columbia River Inter-Tribal Fish Commission, "Nez Perce Tribe."
2. New World Encyclopedia, "Shoshone"; Loether, "Shoshones"; Shoshone-Bannock Tribes.
3. Encyclopedia Britannica, "Boise."
4. Idaho State Historical Society, "Location of Idaho's Territorial Capital."
5. Preston, "Those Dirty Scoundrels Stole the Capital."
6. Ibid.
7. Idaho State Historical Society, "Location of Idaho's Territorial Capital."
8. Gaboury, "Stealing the Seal Was a Capital Move"; Preston, "Those Dirty Scoundrels Stole the Capital."
9. Gaboury, "Stealing the Seal Was a Capital Move."
10. Preston, "Those Dirty Scoundrels Stole the Capital."
11. Gaboury, "Stealing the Seal Was a Capital Move"; Preston, "Those Dirty Scoundrels Stole the Capital."
12. Terry, "Any Ideas Where the Old Seal Might Be?"
13. Columbia River Inter-Tribal Fish Commission, "Nez Perce Tribe."
14. Thatcher, "Bear River Massacre"; Michno, *Deadliest Indian War in the West*; Shoshone-Bannock Tribes.

Part I

15. Ayers, "Death of George Grimes."
16. Ibid.
17. Morrissey, "Western Tall Tale Started Idaho City."
18. Noll, "Southern Idaho Vigilantism," 28.
19. Ibid.; "The Killing of Pinkham," *Walla Walla (ID) Statesman*, August 25, 1865.
20. Noll, "Southern Idaho Vigilantism," 28.
21. "Killing of Pinkham."
22. "Voters," *Idaho Statesman* (Boise, ID), October 8, 1864.
23. Ibid.
24. Noll, "Southern Idaho Vigilantism," 28.
25. "Assassination of Ferd. Patterson," *Walla Walla (WA) Statesman*, February 16, 1865.
26. Noll, "Southern Idaho Vigilantism," 28.
27. Ibid.
28. *Idaho World* (Idaho City, ID), July 29, 1865.
29. Noll, "Southern Idaho Vigilantism," 28–29.
30. "The Trial of Ferdinand J. Patterson, *Idaho World* (Idaho City, ID), November 4, 1865.
31. Ibid.
32. Ibid.
33. Ibid.
34. Ibid.
35. Noll, "Southern Idaho Vigilantism," 29.
36. "Letter from the Mother of Sumner Pinkham," *Idaho Statesman* (Boise, ID), September 30, 1865.
37. "Vigilance Committees in Idaho," *Idaho World* (Idaho City, ID), September 3, 1865.
38. "The Murder of Mr. Pinkham," *Idaho Statesman* (Boise, ID), July 27, 1865.
39. Noll, "Southern Idaho Vigilantism," 29.
40. Ibid.
41. "Wars and Rumors of Wars," *Idaho World* (Idaho City, ID), September 3, 1865.
42. Ibid.
43. Ibid.
44. Ibid.
45. Ibid.

46. "Murder of Mr. Pinkham."

47. Noll, "Southern Idaho Vigilantism," 30; *Idaho World* (Idaho City, ID), November 18, 1865.

48. *Idaho World* (Idaho City, ID), September 3, 1865.

49. "Assassination of Ferd. Patterson."

50. Ibid.

51. Ibid.

52. "The Case of Donahue," *Walla Walla (WA) Statesman*, September 28, 1865.

53. Noll, "Southern Idaho Vigilantism," 31.

54. "Case of Donahue."

55. "Robbery of the Overland Stage," *Idaho Statesman* (Boise, ID), November 10, 1865; Dawson, "Guilt or Innocence of Sheriff David Updyke," 13–14.

56. "Robbery of the Overland Stage."

57. Ibid.

58. Ibid.

59. Ibid.

60. Behm, "Bringing Law and Order to the Boise Basin," 28.

61. "Exact Science," *Idaho Statesman* (Boise, ID), June 27, 1865.

62. Behm, "Bringing Law and Order to the Boise Basin," 28–29.

63. Ibid., 28–29; Noll, "Southern Idaho Vigilantism," 25.

64. Noll, "Southern Idaho Vigilantism," 26.

65. Ibid.

66. Ibid.

67. Behm, "Bringing Law and Order to the Boise Basin," 29.

68. Noll, "Southern Idaho Vigilantism," 27.

69. "Dust Meeting," *Idaho World* (Idaho City, ID), October 14, 1865.

70. "Gold Dust as a Circulating Medium," *Idaho World* (Idaho City, ID), October 9, 1865.

71. Noll, "Southern Idaho Vigilantism," 27.

72. Ibid.

73. Dawson, "Guilt or Innocence of Sheriff David Updyke," 12–13; Behm, "Bringing Law and Order to the Boise Basin," 29.

74. "The Election," *Idaho Statesman* (Boise, ID), March 7, 1865.

75. Dawson, "Guilt or Innocence of Sheriff David Updyke," 13.

76. "The Arrest of Sheriff Updyke—The Charges Against Him," *Idaho Statesman* (Boise, ID), September 30, 1865.

77. Dawson, "Guilt or Innocence of Sheriff David Updyke," 13.

78. "The Sheriff Imbroglio," *Idaho Statesman* (Boise, ID), October 7, 1865.

79. "Volunteers Gone," *Idaho Statesman* (Boise, ID), March 3, 1866; Noll, "Southern Idaho Vigilantism," 31.

80. "Volunteers Gone," *Idaho Statesman* (Boise, ID), March 3, 1866.

81. "Ada: Bruneau: Jennings," *Idaho Statesman* (Boise, ID), March 31, 1866.

82. Noll, "Southern Idaho Vigilantism," 31.

83. Ibid.

84. "Another Chapter of Crime," *Idaho Statesman* (Boise, ID), April 5, 1865.

85. Ibid.

86. Noll, "Southern Idaho Vigilantism," 32.

87. "The Present Condition," *Idaho Statesman* (Boise, ID), April 17, 1866.

88. Dawson, "Guilt or Innocence of Sheriff David Updyke," 16.

89. Ibid., 12.

90. "Governor Lyon: Dr. Ballard," *Idaho Statesman* (Boise, ID), May 12, 1866.

91. "Vigilante Operations and Schemes," *Idaho World* (Idaho City, ID), April 21, 1866.

92. "Present Condition."

93. Dawson, "Guilt or Innocence of Sheriff David Updyke," 16.

94. "Married," *Idaho Statesman* (Boise, ID), October 6, 1866; National Governors Association, "Gov. William John McConnell"; McConnell, *Early History of Idaho.*

95. Noll, "Southern Idaho Vigilantism," 32.

Part II

96. *Idaho Statesman* (Boise, ID), July 29, 1892.

97. Ibid.; "A Sad Case," *Idaho Statesman* (Boise, ID), August 10, 1892.

98. "Sad Case."

99. Ibid.; "A Lively Battle," *Idaho Statesman* (Boise, ID), August 24, 1892.

100. "Warrants Issued," *Idaho Statesman* (Boise, ID), August 12, 1892.

101. "Lively Battle."

102. Ibid.

103. Ibid.

104. Ibid.

105. Ibid.

106. Ibid.

107. "Mrs. Benham Talks," *Idaho Statesman* (Boise, ID), August 25, 1892.

108. Ibid.

109. Ibid.

110. "They Are Not Held," *Idaho Statesman* (Boise, ID), August 26, 1892; *Idaho Statesman* (Boise, ID), August 30, 1892.

111. "Sad Case."

112. "Out of Prison," *Idaho Statesman* (Boise, ID), December 9, 1899.

113. Ibid.

114. Ibid.

115. "In the Supreme Court," *Idaho Statesman* (Boise, ID), January 18, 1895.

116. WSKG, "Civil War and Challenging."

117. Russell, "Necessary Evil," 42.

118. Ibid., 20, 21.

119. Ibid., 18, 26.

120. Ibid., 2, 21.

121. Ibid., 8, 30, 38.

122. Ibid., 49, 51, 53, 64.

123. Ibid., 118–20.

124. Ibid., 51, 53, 59; "Idaho Street Cases in Court," *Idaho Statesman*, September 17, 1889.

125. Russell, "Necessary Evil," 178; Webb, "Death in Levy's Alley," 14, 15.

126. Russell, "Necessary Evil," 114.

127. Russell, "Necessary Evil," 122, 124.

128. Ibid., 121, 122.

129. Webb, "Death in Levy's Alley," 15.

130. Hart, "Well-Liked Businessman."

131. Webb, "Death in Levy's Alley," 15.

132. "Trouble in the Alley," *Idaho Statesman* (Boise, ID), May 10, 1901; "Davis Levy Convicted on Bawdy House Charge," *Idaho Statesman* (Boise, ID), May 11, 1901; Russell, "Necessary Evil," 124.

133. "Trouble in the Alley," *Idaho Statesman*, May 10, 1901; Russell, "Necessary Evil," 124, 126.

134. Russell, "Necessary Evil," 185–86.

135. Ibid., 164–65.

136. Ibid., 178.

137. Webb, "Death in Levy's Alley," 15; Russell, "Necessary Evil," 54, 165, 168, 176.

138. Russell, "Necessary Evil," 165–66.

139. "Idaho Street Cases in Court"; "Guilty as Charged," *Idaho Statesman* (Boise, ID), September 18, 1889; Russell, "Necessary Evil," 58–59.

140. "Shooting at Nampa," *Idaho Statesman* (Boise, ID), June 15, 1890.

141. Ibid.

142. "The Case of Nettie Bowen," *Idaho Statesman* (Boise, ID), June 17, 1890.

143. "Nettie Bowen Held to Answer," *Idaho Statesman* (Boise, ID), July 2, 1890.

144. "Meeting of the Board," *Idaho Statesman* (Boise, ID), July 20, 1890; "Firebugs at Work in Nampa," *Idaho Statesman* (Boise, ID), July 26, 1890; *Idaho Statesman* (Boise, ID), August 3, 1890.

145. "The District Court," *Idaho Statesman* (Boise, ID), March 29, 1891.

146. "Jimmy Turner's Arrest," *Idaho Statesman* (Boise, ID), November 25, 1891.

147. "Jimmy Turner's Arrest"; *Idaho Statesman* (Boise, ID), November 26, 1891.

148. "Jim Turner Stabbed," *Idaho Statesman* (Boise, ID), March 29, 1892; "Local Brevities," *Idaho Statesman* (Boise, ID), April 1, 1892; "In the County Court," *Idaho Statesman* (Boise, ID), April 7, 1892.

149. "Another Raid," *Idaho Statesman* (Boise, ID), August 5, 1892; *Idaho Statesman* (Boise, ID), June 16, 1894; *Idaho Statesman* (Boise, ID), May 1, 1895; *Idaho Statesman* (Boise, ID), July 14, 1896.

150. "Shot at Him: A Notorious Rounder Foiled by an Enraged Female," *Idaho Statesman* (Boise, ID), August 3, 1892.

151. "Wretched Woman Takes Her Life," *Idaho Statesman* (Boise, ID), September 14, 1903.

152. "Ashton Woman Dies," *Idaho Statesman* (Boise, ID), September 15, 1903; "Three Fined in Police Court," *Idaho Statesman* (Boise, ID), September 16, 1903.

153. *Idaho Statesman* (Boise, ID), July 14, 1896; "Shot at Him"; "Wretched Woman Takes Her Life"; "Three Fined in Police Court"; "Ashton Woman Dies"; "Three Fined in Police Court."

154. "Notice," *Idaho Statesman* (Boise, ID), October 12–19, 1904; "Young Woman Dies in Agony," *Idaho Statesman* (Boise, ID), October 19, 1904.

155. Russell, "Necessary Evil," 108, 109; "Three Fined in Police Court."

156. "Davis Levy Foully Murdered," *Idaho Statesman* (Boise, ID), October 6, 1901.

157. "Davis Levy Foully Murdered"; "Very Brutal Act," *Idaho Statesman* (Boise, ID), October 20, 1901; "Officers Search Levy's Office Room," *Idaho Statesman* (Boise, ID), October 7, 1901.

158. Hart, "Levy's 'House of Horrors'"; "Tortured by Fiends," *Idaho Statesman* (Boise, ID), October 9, 1901.

159. Hart, "Levy's 'House of Horrors.'"

160. Ibid.

161. "Davis Levy Foully Murdered"; "Appraisers' Work," *Idaho Statesman* (Boise, ID), October 20, 1901.

162. Just, "Levy, Levy, and Levy's Alley"; "Officers Search Levy's Office Room"; "Murder of Levy," *Idaho Statesman* (Boise, ID), October 8, 1901; "Proved an Alibi," *Idaho Statesman* (Boise, ID), October 10, 1901.

163. "Arrested for Levy Murder," *Idaho Statesman* (Boise, ID), October 22, 1901.

164. Ibid.; "Joe Levy in Court," *Idaho Statesman* (Boise, ID), October 24, 1901; "Murder the Charge," *Idaho Statesman* (Boise, ID), October 23, 1901; Just, "Levy, Levy, and Levy's Alley."

165. Webb, "Death in Levy's Alley," 16; "Levy Murder Case," *Idaho Statesman* (Boise, ID), October 6, 1901; "Murder of Levy."

166. "Bound Over to District Court," *Idaho Statesman* (Boise, ID), November 6, 1901; "George Levy Makes a Scene in the Jail," *Idaho Statesman* (Boise, ID), November 7, 1901.

167. "Edelburg Insane," *Idaho Statesman* (Boise, ID), November 18, 1901; "Edelburg Adjudged Insane," *Idaho Statesman* (Boise, ID), November 19, 1901.

168. "Frenchman Levy Found Guilty," *Idaho Statesman* (Boise, ID), February 21, 1902; Just, "Levy, Levy, and Levy's Alley."

169. Just, "Levy, Levy, and Levy's Alley."

Part III

170. Schock, "Demorest Medal."

171. Baker, "Levi's Alley."

172. History, "Woman's Christian Temperance Union"; The Ohio State University College of Arts and Sciences, "Anti-Saloon League"; PBS, "Distilled."

173. Irish, "Second Great Awakening."

174. "Reform Measures to Be Introduced," *Idaho Statesman* (Boise, ID), January 12, 1907.

175. "Sunday Rest Law Indorsed," *Idaho Statesman* (Boise, ID), February 4, 1907; "Sunday Rest Law in Operation Today," *Idaho Statesman* (Boise, ID), May 12, 1907.

176. "Sunday Rest Law in Operation Today."

177. Ibid.

178. "Sunday Law Delays Harvest," *Idaho Statesman* (Boise, ID), August 6, 1907; "New Attack on the Sunday Rest Law," *Idaho Statesman* (Boise, ID), August 18, 1907; Just, "Little Slice of History."

179. "Prohibition Is the End Sought," *Idaho Statesman* (Boise, ID), May 14, 1908.

180. Alcohol Problems and Solutions, "Local Option Alcohol Laws in the US."

181. "Local Option Is Recommended by Senate," *Idaho Statesman* (Boise, ID), February 10, 1909; "Preparing to Make Idaho 'Dry,'" *Idaho Statesman* (Boise, ID), February 18, 1909.

182. "Accepts Challenge of Liquor Interests," *Idaho Statesman* (Boise, ID), August 31, 1901.

183. "Saloons Close Voluntarily," *Idaho Statesman* (Boise, ID), September 5, 1909.

184. "Prohibition Hurts Business," *Idaho Statesman* (Boise, ID), September 1, 1909.

185. "Issue Now Is Up to Voters of County," *Idaho Statesman* (Boise, ID), September 8, 1909.

186. "Cassie County Dry by Large Majority," *Idaho Statesman* (Boise, ID), December 2, 1909; "'Dry' Majority Small," *Idaho Statesman* (Boise, ID), December 9, 1909; "New Lease on Life," *Idaho Statesman* (Boise, ID), October 26, 1909.

187. "Pence Removes Reeves and Davis," *Idaho Statesman* (Boise, ID), October 2, 1909.

188. "All Work for Boise," *Idaho Statesman* (Boise, ID), September 13, 1909.

189. "Woman Pleads for Dry Idaho," *Idaho Statesman* (Boise, ID), October 30, 1916.

190. "Liquor Forces Busy in Idaho," *Idaho Statesman* (Boise, ID), July 14, 1916.

191. "Idaho Is Dry by 3 to 1 Vote," *Idaho Statesman* (Boise, ID), November 30, 1916.

192. "Whisky Consumed in 1916 Greater than in Any Year Since 1909," *Idaho Statesman* (Boise, ID), January 15, 1917.

193. "Detectives Raid Sleeper," *Idaho Statesman* (Boise, ID), January 26, 1917.

194. "Pullman-Auto Booze Seizure," *Idaho Statesman* (Boise, ID), April 4, 1917; "Cole Held Not Guilty for Breaking Liquor Law," *Idaho Statesman* (Boise, ID), August 4, 1917.

195. "Booze, Autos, and Men Taken," *Idaho Statesman* (Boise, ID), May 30, 1917.

196. "Booze Cached in City Limits," *Idaho Statesman* (Boise, ID), August 21, 1917; "Bootleggers Are Arrested," *Idaho Statesman* (Boise, ID), August 18, 1917.

197. "Tucker Under Charge of Shipping in Booze," *Idaho Statesman* (Boise, ID), June 11, 1918.

198. "Lingerie and Booze Found Inside Trunk," *Idaho Statesman* (Boise, ID), January 7, 1917.

199. "Booze Cached in Ditch," *Idaho Statesman* (Boise, ID), July 24, 1917.

200. "Coyote Digs Up 44 Quarts of Real," *Idaho Statesman* (Boise, ID), May 16, 1917.

201. "Accuse Prisoner of Taking Booze," *Idaho Statesman* (Boise, ID), April 13, 1918.

202. "Cora Gaskell in Custody," *Idaho Statesman* (Boise, ID), July 4, 1918.

203. "Policewoman Is in Toils of Law," *Idaho Statesman* (Boise, ID), April 17, 1919; "Mrs. Gaskill Pleads Guilty to Booze Charge Before Judge Reddoch," *Idaho Statesman* (Boise, ID), June 12, 1919.

204. "Boise Courts," *Idaho Statesman* (Boise, ID), June 12, 1919; "Mrs. Gaskell Given Thirty Days in Jail," *Idaho Statesman* (Boise, ID), June 19, 1919.

205. Lerner, "Unintended Consequences."

206. "City and County Officials Named in Liquor Intrigue," *Idaho Statesman* (Boise, ID), February 13, 1923.

207. Ibid.

208. "Nine Deny Guilt on Liquor Charge," *Idaho Statesman* (Boise, ID), February 15, 1923.

209. "Conspiracy Case Defense Applies for Particulars," *Idaho Statesman* (Boise, ID), February 22, 1923; "Trial of Accused Officers to Open at 9:30 Today," *Idaho Statesman* (Boise, ID), February 26, 1923.

210. "U.S. Says Boise Physician Chief of Liquor Ring," *Idaho Statesman* (Boise, ID), February 28, 1923.

211. "U.S Charges Boise Doctor 'Brains' of Bootleggers' Ring," *Idaho Statesman* (Boise, ID), February 28, 1923; "U.S. Says Boise Physician Chief of Liquor Ring."

212. "U.S Charges Boise Doctor 'Brains' of Bootleggers' Ring."

213. "U.S. Says Boise Physician Chief of Liquor Ring."

214. "Dr. H. Goodfriend Called to Stand by His Attorney," *Idaho Statesman* (Boise, ID), March 3, 1923.

215. "Dr. H. Goodfriend Call to Stand at Night Session," *Idaho Statesman* (Boise, ID), March 3, 1923.

216. Ibid.

217. "Dr. H. Goodfriend Called to Stand by His Attorney."

218. "Dr. H. Goodfriend Call to Stand at Night Session."

219. Ibid.

220. "Jury Finds Six Guilty After Six Hours of Debate," *Idaho Statesman* (Boise, ID), March 4, 1923.

221. Ibid.

222. Ibid.

223. "Sentences Are Given Six on Booze Charge," *Idaho Statesman* (Boise, ID), April 10, 1923.
224. Lerner, "Unintended Consequences."
225. Ibid.
226. Ibid.; Philips, "Jake-Leg Epidemic."

Part IV

227. Branham, "Saints Were Sinners."
228. Ibid.
229. PBS, "Anti-Mormon Violence."
230. George and Saunders, "Republicans and the Relics of Barbarism."
231. Branham, "Saints Were Sinners."
232. Davis, "Edmunds Act of 1882."
233. "District Court," *Idaho Statesman*, May 7, 1916; "District Court," *Idaho Statesman*, September 10, 1916; Idaho State Penitentiary, Parole Agreement, Edward Cooper, December 21, 1916.
234. Waxman, "This Is What Americans Used to Consider Obscene."
235. U.S. Department of Justice, "Citizen's Guide to U.S. Federal Law."
236. "Held by Commissioner Brown," *Idaho Statesman*, August 27, 1891; "A Negro Indicted," *Idaho Statesman*, November 19, 1891; Idaho State Penitentiary, Description of Convict, Mike Kirby, November 28, 1891; Idaho State Penitentiary, Description of Convict, James Clark, February 3, 1892.
237. Krusei, "Rarely Used Adultery Charge."
238. "Law-Turpin Case from Star Heard," *Idaho Statesman*, November 18, 1905.
239. Ibid.; "Judge Tempers Justice with Mercy," *Idaho Statesman*, December 19, 1905.
240. "Judge Tempers Justice with Mercy."
241. Krusei, "Rarely Used Adultery Charge."
242. "Sentenced to Serve Time in State Prison," *Idaho Statesman*, November 20, 1920; Idaho State Penitentiary, exhibit, "Faces of the Idaho State Penitentiary."
243. "Two Boise Men Held by Police in Morals Case," *Idaho Statesman*, March 31, 1959; Idaho State Penitentiary, exhibit, "Faces of the Idaho State Penitentiary"; "Morals Charge Nets Boisean Prison Term," *Idaho Statesman*, July 30, 1959.

244. Adkins, "These People Are Frightened to Death."

245. Randal and Virta, "Idaho's Original Same-Sex Scandal."

246. Harvard Business School, "Women and the Law"; Silverberg, "History of Women and Money"; Idaho State Historical Society, "Leading the Way."

247. Silverberg, "History of Women and Money"; Barroso and Brown, "Gender Pay Gap in the U.S."

248. Shallat and Beierle, *Numbered*, 122; State of Idaho Department of Public Health, Division of Vital Statistics, Certificate of Divorce, 1191, *Mary Klingensmith v. Harry Klingensmith*, Ada County, August 2, 1954.

249. Shallat and Beierle, *Numbered*, 123.

250. Idaho State Penitentiary, #5231—Mary J. Mills Biography.

251. Idaho State Penitentiary, Mary J. Mills file, December 30, 1935.

252. Ibid.

253. Idaho State Penitentiary, Mary J. Mills file; Shallat and Beierle, *Numbered*, 57.

254. "Mrs. Lacey Will Learn Fate Friday," *Idaho Statesman*, April 19, 1949.

255. Ibid.; Centers for Disease Control and Prevention, "Facts About Strychnine."

256. "Mrs. Lacey Will Learn Fate Friday."

257. Ibid.,; "Attorney Files Formal Charge Against Matron," *Idaho Statesman*, April 16, 1949.

258. "Mrs. Lacey Will Learn Fate Friday."

259. Lottie Ashdown was booked into the Idaho State Penitentiary under the name "Elizabeth Lacey," suggesting that she hadn't changed her legal name since marrying and divorcing her second husband.

260. Shallat and Beierle, *Numbered*, 122.

261. "Woman Tells Court Husband Tried to Blackmail," *Idaho Statesman*, May 7, 1908.

262. Ibid.

263. Ibid.

264. Ibid.

265. Ibid.

266. Ibid.

267. Shallat and Beierle, *Numbered*, 32.

268. "Principals in the Sensational Daly Murder," *Idaho Statesman*, October 16, 1904; "Murdered in His Own Home," *Idaho Statesman*, October 7, 1904.

269. "Principals in the Sensational Daly Murder."

270. "Murdered in His Own Home."

271. Ibid.

272. Ibid.

273. Ibid.

274. "Murdered in His Own Home"; "Must Answer for Murder," *Idaho Statesman*, October 8, 1904.

275. "Bond Begins to Weaken," *Idaho Statesman*, October 9, 1904.

276. Ibid.

277. "Widow Held as an Accomplice," *Idaho Statesman*, October 15, 1904.

278. "Standing Room at a Premium," *Idaho Statesman*, February 11, 1905.

279. "Mrs. Daly Is Star Witness," *Idaho Statesman*, February 12, 1905.

280. Ibid.

281. "Sticks Firmly to Her Story," *Idaho Statesman*, February 14, 1905; "Must Answer for Murder."

282. "Sticks Firmly to Her Story"; "Murder in the First Degree," *Idaho Statesman*, February 16, 1905; "Bond to Hang on April 14," *Idaho Statesman*, February 19, 1905.

283. "Trial of Mrs. Daly Is Begun," *Idaho Statesman*, February 21, 1905; "Story of Mrs. Daly's Career," *Idaho Statesman*, February 22, 1905.

284. "Story of Mrs. Daly's Career"; "Murdered in His Own Home."

285. "Story of Mrs. Daly's Career."

286. "Is Guilty of Manslaughter," *Idaho Statesman*, February 23, 1905.

287. "Must Serve Ten Years in Prison," *Idaho Statesman*, February 26, 1905.

288. "Bond Pays the Death Penalty for Murder of Charles Daly," *Idaho Statesman*, August 11, 1906.

289. "Jennie Daly Doesn't Care," *Idaho Statesman*, August 12, 1906.

290. "Jennie Daly Doesn't Care"; "Leaves for Old Home," *Idaho Statesman*, June 11, 1911.

Epilogue

291. Dawson, "Judge Says Idaho Can't Force."

292. Slisco, "Idaho Being Sued"; Dawson, "Judge Says Idaho Can't Force."

293. Official Guide to Government Information and Services, "U.S. Department of Justice," https://www.usa.gov/federal-agencies/u-s-department-of-justice.

294. Van Hyning, "These Idaho Cities"; Boone, "Census."

BIBLIOGRAPHY

PRIMARY SOURCES

Idaho State Penitentiary. "Faces of the Idaho State Penitentiary." Accessed August 21, 2020.

Idaho State Penitentiary. Inmate files.

Idaho Statesman (Boise, Idaho).

Idaho World (Idaho City, Idaho).

State of Idaho Department of Public Health, Division of Vital Statistics.

Walla Walla (WA) Statesman.

SECONDARY SOURCES

Adkins, Judith. "'These People Are Frightened to Death': Congressional Investigations and the Lavender Scare." *Prologue Magazine* 48, no 2. (Summer 2016). https://www.archives.gov/publications/prologue/2016/summer/lavender.html.

Alcohol Problems and Solutions. "Local Option Alcohol Laws in the US: History and Status." https://www.alcoholproblemsandsolutions.org/local-option-alcohol-laws-in-the-u-s.

Ayers, Jesse L. "The Death of George Grimes." *Idaho Magazine.* https://www.idahomagazine.com/article/the-death-of-george-grimes.

Baker, Arthur. "Levi's Alley: Early Boise's Red Light Area." *Idaho Statesman*, November 13, 1978.

Barroso, Amanda, and Anna Brown. "Gender Pay Gap in the U.S. Held Steady in 2020." Pew Research Center, May 25, 2021. https://www.pewresearch.org/fact-tank/2021/05/25/gender-pay-gap-facts.

Behm, Connie. "Bringing Law and Order to the Boise Basin." *Boise Magazine* (Spring 1985).

Boone, Rebecca. "Census: Meridian One of 10 Fastest-Growing U.S. Cities." KTVB, August 13, 2021. https://www.ktvb.com/article/news/local/growing-idaho/census-meridian-one-of-10-fastest-growing-us-cities-idaho-growth-census/277-5650756a-2c10-43c3-b1b3-87e6c45bb650.

Branham, Colin. "The Saints Were Sinners: The Mormon Question and the Survival of Idaho." Boise State University. https://www.boisestate.edu/presidents-writing-awards/the-saints-were-sinnersthe-mormon-question-and-the-survival-of-idaho.

Centers for Disease Control and Prevention. "Facts About Strychnine." https://emergency.cdc.gov/agent/strychnine/basics/facts.asp.

Columbia Inter-Tribal Fish Commission. "Nez Perce Tribe." https://www.critfc.org/member_tribes_overview/nez-perce-tribe.

Davis, Jenna. "The Edmunds Act of 1882." Utah Communication History Encyclopedia (Spring 2017). https://utahcommhistory.com/2017/04/27/the-edmunds-act-of-1882.

Dawson, Alson William. "The Guilt or Innocence of Sheriff David Updyke." *Boise Vision*, December 1980.

Dawson, James. "Judge Says Idaho Can't Force 2 Men to Register as Sex Offenders for 'Crimes Against Nature.'" Boise State Public Radio, September 9, 2021. https://www.boisestatepublicradio.org/law-justice/2021-09-09/judge-says-idaho-cant-force-2-men-to-register-as-sex-offenders-for-crimes-against-nature.

Encyclopedia Britannica. "Boise." https://www.britannica.com/place/Boise-Idaho.

Gaboury, Kevin. "Stealing the Seal Was a Capital Move." *Lewiston Tribune*, August 5, 2011. https://lmtribune.com/northwest/stealing-the-seal-was-a-capital-move/article_037c8262-44eb-5833-aa78-3f08a6d1cc67.html.

George, Robert P., and William L. Saunders. "Republicans and the Relics of Barbarism." National Review, August 30, 2004. https://www.nationalreview.com/2004/08/republicans-and-relics-barbarism-robert-p-george-william-l-saunders.

Hart, Arthur. "Levy's 'House of Horrors' Sparks Campaign for Reform." *Idaho Statesman*, July 25, 2010.

———. "Well-Liked Businessman Becomes 'Miserly Scoundrel.'" *Idaho Statesman*, July 18, 2010.

Harvard Business School. "Women and the Law." https://www.library.hbs.edu/hc/wes/collections/women_law.

History. "Woman's Christian Temperance Union." August 21, 2018. https://www.history.com/topics/womens-history/womans-christian-temperance-union.

Idaho State Historical Society. "Leading the Way: Idaho Women and the Vote." Women's Suffrage in Idaho. https://history.idaho.gov/2020-suffrage-exhibit.

———. "Location of Idaho's Territorial Capital." Reference Series, no. 344, December 24, 1964. https://history.idaho.gov/wp-content/uploads/0344_Location-of-Idahos-Territorial-Capital.pdf.

Irish, Kerry. "The Second Great Awakening and the Making of Modern America." 2018. https://digitalcommons.georgefox.edu/cgi/viewcontent.cgi?article=1077&context=hist_fac.

Just, Rick. "Levy, Levy, and Levy's Alley." RickJust, October 18, 2018. https://www.rickjust.com/blog/levy-levy-and-levys-alley.

———. "A Little Slice of History: Sunday Rest." *Idaho Press*, April 19, 2020. https://www.idahopress.com/community/community_columns/a-little-slice-of-history-sunday-rest/article_43e3e3ee-90bc-59b5-b163-11bfaacaca2d.html.

Krusei, Kimberly. "Rarely Used Adultery Charge Still a Felony in Idaho." KTVB, September 4, 2016. https://www.ktvb.com/article/news/crime/rarely-used-adultery-charge-still-a-felony-in-idaho/277-313480032.

Lerner, Michael. "Unintended Consequences." From *Prohibition*, a film by Ken Burns and Lynn Novick. PBS. https://www.pbs.org/kenburns/prohibition/unintended-consequences.

Lister, Kate. "Sex Workers or Prostitutes? Why Words Matter." iNews, October 5, 2017. https://inews.co.uk/opinion/columnists/sex-workers-prostitutes-words-matter-95447.

Loether, Christopher. "Shoshones." Plains Humanities Alliance. http://plainshumanities.unl.edu/encyclopedia/doc/egp.na.105.

McConnell, William John. *Early History of Idaho*. Caldwell, ID: Caxton Press, 1913.

Michno, Gregory. *The Deadliest Indian War in the West: The Snake Conflict, 1864–1868*. Caldwell, ID: Caxton Press, 2007.

Morrissey, David. "Western Tall Tale Started Idaho City." *Lewiston Morning Tribune*, March 19, 1976.

National Governors Association. "Gov. William John McConnell." Last modified 2020. https://www.nga.org/governor/william-john-mcconnell.

New World Encyclopedia. "Shoshone." https://www.newworldencyclopedia.org/entry/shoshone.

Noll, Lowell H. "Southern Idaho Vigilantism." *Pacific Northwesterner* 2, no. 2 (1957).

The Ohio State University College of Arts and Sciences. "Anti-Saloon League." Temperance and Prohibition, 2021. https://prohibition.osu.edu/anti-saloon-league.

PBS. "Anti-Mormon Violence." American Experience. https://www.pbs.org/wgbh/americanexperience/features/mormons-opposition.

———. "Distilled: A History of Idaho's Alcohol Laws." January 22, 2018.

Philips, Mary. "Jake-Leg Epidemic First Reported by Oklahoma City Doctors." *The Oklahoman*, June 14, 2013. https://www.oklahoman.com/article/3849680/jake-leg-epidemic-first-reported-by-oklahoma-city-doctors.

Preston, Seth. "Those Dirty Scoundrels Stole the Capital." *Lewiston Tribune*, July, 3, 1990.

Randal, Seth, and Alan Virta. "Idaho's Original Same-Sex Scandal." *New York Times*, September 2, 2007. https://www.nytimes.com/2007/09/02/opinion/02randal.html.

Russell, Jo Anne. "A Necessary Evil: Prostitutes, Patriarchs, and Profits in Boise City, 1863–1915." Master's thesis, Boise State University, 1991.

Schock, Barbara. "The Demorest Medal." Carl Sundburg Historic Site Association, March 3, 2014. https://www.sandburg.org/SandburgsHometown/SandburgsHometown_DemorestMedal.html.

Shallat, Todd, and Amber Beierle. *Numbered*. Boise: Idaho State Historical Society, 2020.

Shoshone-Bannock Tribes. http://www.sbtribes.com.

Silverberg, Tiffany. "The History of Women and Money in the United States in Honor of Women's History Month." https://www.oneadvisorypartners.com/blog/the-history-of-women-and-money-in-the-united-states-in-honor-of-womens-history-month.

Slisco, Aila. "Idaho Being Sued for Anti-Gay 'Crimes Against Nature' Law." *Newsweek*, September 29, 2020. https://www.newsweek.com/idaho-being-sued-anti-gay-crimes-against-nature-law-1534788.

Terry, Marlene. "Any Ideas Where the Old Seal Might Be?" *Idaho Press*, February 7, 2013. https://www.idahopress.com/members/any-ideas-where-the-old-seal-might-be/article_53436f1c-70c5-11e2-a806-001a4bcf887a.html.

Thatcher, Elaine. "The Bear River Massacre." Utah Humanities. https://www.utahhumanities.org/stories/items/show/258.

U.S. Department of Justice "Citizen's Guide to U.S. Federal Law on Obscenity." May 28. 2020. https://www.justice.gov/criminal-ceos/citizens-guide-us-federal-law-obscenity.

Van Hyning, Celina. "These Idaho Cities Had the Fastest U.S. Growth Rate Between 2019–2020." KTVB, June 14, 2021. https://www.ktvb.com/article/news/local/growing-idaho/idaho-growth-migration-cities-2020-data/277-cbe99c0c-712f-43f7-8979-4583ced1589e.

Waxman, Olivia B. "This Is What Americans Used to Consider Obscene." *Time*, June 21, 2016. https://time.com/4373765/history-obscenity-united-states-films-miller-ulysses-roth.

Webb, Anna. "Death in Levy's Alley," *Boise Weekly*, November 5–11, 1998.

WSKG. "The Civil War and Challenging the 'Cult of True Womanhood.'" February 11, 2016. https://wskg.org/history/the-civil-war-and-challenging-the-cult-of-true-womanhood.

ABOUT THE AUTHOR

*J*anelle M. Scheffelmaier is an independent historian, researcher, writer, avid reader, and lifelong learner. Janelle holds a Bachelor of Arts in English from the University of Montana and a Master of Arts in History from Norwich University. Janelle is passionate about storytelling. She loves hearing and telling powerful stories, real and imagined, that offer insight into the best and worst—but especially the best—humanity has to offer.

Janelle was born and raised in the Idaho Panhandle. She lives in Boise and enjoys exploring the mountains with her daughter and their over-energetic dog. She currently has two novels in draft form and is usually trying to read at least three books at one time. She is the author of *Butte and the 1918 Influenza Pandemic*.